T0265681

DEFIANT HOPE, ACTIVE LOVE

DEFIANT HOPE, ACTIVE LOVE

WHAT YOUNG ADULTS ARE SEEKING IN PLACES OF WORK, FAITH, AND COMMUNITY

EDITED BY
Jeffrey F. Keuss

WILLIAM B. EERDMANS PUBLISHING COMPANY
GRAND RAPIDS, MICHIGAN

Wm. B. Eerdmans Publishing Co.
4035 Park East Court SE, Grand Rapids, Michigan 49546
www.eerdmans.com

30 29 28 27 26 25 24   1 2 3 4 5 6 7

ISBN 978-0-8028-8391-9

Library of Congress Cataloging-in-Publication Data

A catalog record for this book is available from the Library
of Congress.

Unless otherwise noted, Scripture quotations are taken from
the New Revised Standard Version, Updated Edition.

Contents

CONTENTS

Introduction

Faithful Spaces

The Changing Shape of Community

JEFFREY F. KEUSS

Unless I read the evidence wrongly, the political and philosophic history of the West during the past 150 years can be understood as a series of attempts—more or less conscious, more or less systematic, more or less violent—to fill the central emptiness left by the erosion of theology. This vacancy, this darkness in the middle, was one of "the death of God" ... but I think we could put it more accurately: the decay of a comprehensive Christian doctrine had left in disorder, or had left blank, essential perceptions of social justice, of the meaning of human history, of the relations between mind and body, of the place of knowledge in our moral conduct.

—George Steiner[1]

1. *Nostalgia for the Absolute* (Toronto, ON: House of Anansi Press, 1974), 1–2.

The Forest and the Trees

On the Olympic Peninsula in Washington State near the Hoh Rain Forest stands a grove of trees that constitute a part of one of the most pristine and calm locations on the planet. Considered by some scientists as the quietest place on Earth due to the lack of noise pollution from any human development, the Hoh Rain Forest is a place where the sounds that you do hear as you stand in the quiet come from subtle and constant growth at all levels. The dripping of water sinking into the rich soil, the sounds of birds and ground animals of all sorts making their way to and fro, the creak and rustle of branches from western red cedars towering over a hundred feet in the air—trees that have been growing for over a century. Once you quiet your mind and soul and are just present in this dense, quiet space, you feel growth all around you. It is like walking in the midst of life itself as it is renewed and strengthened. Yet a few hundred miles southeast from this pristine setting is another grove that tells a different story. In the Wanapum Recreation Area near Vantage on the Columbia River stands a grove of ginkgo trees. These ancient trees, like the western red cedars in the Hoh Rain Forest, have stood the test of time. Yet as you draw close to these silent timeless sentinels, you will notice very quickly that rather than having life and life abundantly, these trees are hard as stone. You will notice a slight discoloration to the bark and the flora around the base will be eerily absent—no ferns, no mosses. When you touch these trees, they will be cold and hard under your hand, absorbing your warmth rather than giving you comfort from another living thing. These trees were once alive, like the hundreds of other trees that populate the "Evergreen State," but due to a shift in mineral deposits underground, the runoff from the surrounding Columbia River Gorge gradually caused the water table that fed the root structures to become toxic. The trees, being unable to move, continued to drink what they were given. Over time the ginkgoes took in so much of these minerals that the old adage "you are what you eat" proved true, and they became literal rocks shaped like their former living selves.

Perhaps there is no better analogy for the current state of faith communities in the twenty-first century, not only in the Pacific Northwest but on a global scale. When I was a professor in Scotland, I could drive through any city or village and see the spires of old churches peppering the skyline. When I drove to them I would see the historic architecture, the stained glass, the large doors of the nave—but the sign in front would tell a different story: it might now be a bank, a pub, or even a set of converted high-priced flats. What were once living, breathing faith communities have now become something else entirely. While not always cold and hard to the touch, it was still only a shadowy form of its former purpose. Yet even though the petrification process persists, and even though young adults are leaving faith communities by the thousands each year, there are still some who will walk up to these former titans of faith formation, lay their hands on the stone and brick, and whisper prayers that some resurrection might occur and reanimate these spaces. Often the petitions are framed around the past glory in the form of a certain nostalgia about place and what a space of gathering can and should provide in churches today.

If you are coming to this book in hopes that stone trees will return to life, you should perhaps stop reading here because this is not a book of fairy tales. In short, this is a book that will hopefully provide a clear and honest assessment of what young adults hunger and thirst for in today's world and how faith communities, if they can let go of petrified and fossilized nostalgia and the need to control, might find that faithful spaces still have much to offer young adults. Communities just need the eyes to see and the ears to hear.

Faithful Spaces

After the recent pandemic and the subsequent global isolation, what it means to regather as a people in a place is being radically reimagined, and young adults are on the front lines of the new normal as to what and how community is found, created, and sustained. Our work with thousands of young adults has revealed a growing interest in gathering in community that has a deep and evident call to faithfulness. In her magisterial work *Roman Faith and Christian Faith: Pistis and Fides in the Early Roman Empire and Early Churches*,[2] Teresa Morgan traces the divergence and convergence of how the concept of being in faithful spaces clashed and evolved between secular and sacred communities. What it meant to have faith in the Roman senate or the Praetorian Guard was not the same type of "faith" that one would have in the early church worship spaces or when gathering with other Christians in households (*kat' oikon*, Acts 2:46) as mentioned in Acts 2:42 ("They devoted themselves to the apostles' teaching and to fellowship, to the breaking of bread and to prayer"). Yet as time has moved on, what it means to have faith and find faith in a community and place has become harder and harder to determine. For some, faithfulness and faithful spaces are truly a thing of the past, and what remains is merely the hunger and longing for true faith in the places of work, family, community, and even religious practices. George Steiner's bold pronouncement during his CBC Massey Lectures in some senses anticipates our current moment as he sought to place the question of God back at the center of discourse in the modern conceptions of community building. Elaborating on what he terms as a boundless "nostalgia for the absolute," Steiner states that:

> The major mythologies constructed in the West since the early nineteenth century are not only attempts to fill the emptiness left by the decay of Christian theology and Christian dogma. They are a kind of *substitute theology*. They are systems of belief and argument which may be savagely anti-religious, which may postulate a world without God and may deny an afterlife, but whose

2. Teresa Morgan, *Roman Faith and Christian Faith: Pistis and Fides in the Early Roman Empire and Early Churches* (Oxford: Oxford University Press, 2017).

structure, whose aspirations, whose claims on the believer, are profoundly religious in strategy and effect.[3]

This book is an attempt to name some of the ramifications of this substitute theology that young adults are being asked to embrace today and the effects it is having on their sense of resiliency and commitment to faith communities.

Born from quantitative and qualitative research funded through the Lilly Endowment, the Pivot NW Research team has had the gift of sitting with diverse faith communities and young adults over the years to listen and learn about what their deep needs and desires are for community— not only when it comes to churches and faith-based nonprofits but also regarding the conception of what makes workplaces, families, and civil society meaningful and generative. We began our work prior to the pandemic and have journeyed with these young adults through COVID-19 and now into the postpandemic world. To say that we have learned a lot is a vast understatement. We have heard the clear and present desire for faith to mean something, for churches and faith communities to embrace and uphold the lives of young adults in real ways, and for the calls for justice heard in our streets to find some purchase in the ways communities organize and actualize themselves for the sake of others.

The Big Sort

The mineralized waters that have been petrifying faith communities have been drawn into the root structure for some time as a "substitute theology," to use Steiner's term. Some of this has come about in the long, protracted sorting of class and wealth that Bill Bishop identified more than a decade ago in his landmark book *The Big Sort: Why the Clustering of Like-Minded Americans Is Tearing Us Apart*[4] and gives

3. Steiner, *Nostalgia for the Absolute*, 4.
4. Bill Bishop, *The Big Sort: Why the Clustering of Like-Minded Americans Is Tearing Us Apart* (Boston, MA: Mariner Books, 2009).

further evidence of a substitute theology that drifts away from the faithful spaces that the early Christians imagined. This "big sort" is seen in the great divide that separates the "cognitive elite" and lower class Charles Murray brings to light in *Coming Apart*.[5] He highlights four sociological shifts—the decline of marriage, work ethic, respect for the law and of religious observance—and he meticulously chronicles and measures the emergence of two wholly distinct classes in today's America: a new upper class, first identified in his earlier book *The Bell Curve* as "the cognitive elite" in the imagined town of Belmont, and a new "lower class" personified in his fictive Fishtown.[6] While the sociological assessment offered by Murray is rich in his book *The Bell Curve*, his typological use of the towns of Belmont and Fishtown begs the question: do the cities that Murray imagines represent the fait accompli for deep community in the twenty-first century? In Murray's analysis there is the assumption that cities as we have experienced them will remain the places where deep community will be located and sustained, usually with an eye to a nostalgic past—a "nostalgia for the absolute."[7] Robert Putnam's *Our Kids: The American Dream in Crisis*[8] offers up a similar sepia-toned sentimentality in his nostalgic recollection of 1950s Port Clinton, Ohio, which is a baseline set for his study. While he acknowledges many of its troubles, it was for Putnam "a passable embodiment of the American Dream, a place that offered decent opportunity for all the kids in the town, whatever their background."[9] Yet as we will hear from Ta-Nehisi Coates later in the introduction, perhaps it is the very concept

5. Charles Murray, *Coming Apart: The State of White America, 1960–2010* (New York: Crown Forum, 2012).

6. Charles Murray, *The Bell Curve: Intelligence and Class Structure in American Life* (Free Press, 1994).

7. Steiner, *Nostalgia for the Absolute*.

8. Robert D. Putnam, *Our Kids: The American Dream in Crisis* (New York: Simon & Schuster, 2015).

9. Putnam, *Our Kids*, 1.

and form of the Dream that is the problem to begin with. The young adults we have surveyed and been in relationship with over our years of work certainly say this claim is something to attend to. This form of the idealized city—seen as an Edenic place that can and should be recovered from yesteryear—is evident in much of what passes for solutions to our "coming apart" as a nation that is every day becoming more and more devoid of the faith that so many young adults hunger and thirst for. This dream of a utopia is haunting to many, but is "place" the real issue in and of itself? Rabbi Abraham Heschel made the astute observation in his classic text *The Sabbath*:

> The Bible is more concerned with time than with space. It sees the world in the dimension of time. It pays more attention to generations, to events, than to countries, to things; it is more concerned with history than with geography. To understand the teaching of the Bible, one must accept its premise that time has meaning for life, which is at least equal to that of space; that time has a significance and sovereignty of its own.[10]

For Heschel, Western culture has for too long been obsessed with the colonization of place: "Technical civilization stems primarily from the desire of man to subdue and manage the forces of nature. The manufacture of tools, the art of spinning and farming, the building of houses, the craft of sailing—all this goes on in man's spatial surroundings. The mind's preoccupation with things of space affects, to this day, all activities of man."[11] In this way our control and management of spaces and places becomes idolatrous. Buildings, streets, and the very cities we live in provoke "blindness to all reality that fails to identify itself as a thing, as a matter of fact. This is obvious in

10. Abraham Joshua Heschel, *The Sabbath* (New York: Farrar, Straus & Giroux, 1951), 6–7.
11. Heschel, *The Sabbath*, 4.

our understanding of time, which, being thingless and insubstantial, appears to us as if it had no reality."[12]

Consider our relation to border control and immigration in the early part of the twenty-first century. In what ways were the physical borders of this country and the evocation of "building a wall" lifted to prophetic responsibility akin to the post-exilic call of the prophet Zechariah? As we look on the years that have passed since 9/11, we are continually haunted by the failure of the grand images of America's modern cities—images of busy streets populated with new dreams and visions, soaring skyscrapers reaching to the heavens, and always the unbounded promise of possibilities to be realized. Yet 9/11 offered up the futility of tying our identity to the cities we had constructed. For Americans who collectively watched the Twin Towers collapse into nothingness with clouds of dust chasing once-confident citizens into disarray, it was the death of the modern dream of limitless progress, which had served the country well since the end of World War II. In many respects, this trauma mirrors the response to the 2016 presidential election, with New York City once again the site of confusion, anger, and righteous indignation focused not on Ground Zero but on Trump Tower.

Faithful Space as "Monasticism without Walls"

When one thinks of models for deep faithfulness within the milieu of today's multicultural city and how young adults are seeking to make community and find meaning, the name Thomas Merton does not readily come to mind. As a key figure in modern discourse surrounding Christian spirituality in the twentieth century, Thomas Merton is often remembered as the contemplative critic who left behind the din and clang of New York City for the pastoral cloistered life of a Trappist monastery in Kentucky. However, a closer reading of Merton's life and writing reveals not only a deep concern for the challenges of urban life and multicultural engagement in the context of mid-

---

12. Heschel, *The Sabbath*, 5.

twentieth-century Western culture, but also a voice that provides a provocative vision for our lives in the twenty-first century. Merton is a helpful companion in reading Murray's *Coming Apart* and Putnam's *Our Kids*. For Merton, the monastic life was not an escape or refuge from the modern city but a prophetic form of spirituality that he offered to the "urban uncloistered" time and time again. His calling to the monastic life was as much a profession of faith as it was a compelling alternative paradigm that looked deep into the assertions of material secularism found in city life and called for a renewal of body and spirit that continues to challenge and provoke. As Merton wrote in "Contemplation in a World of Action," "as long as I imagine that the world is something to be 'escaped' in the monastery—that wearing that quaint costume and following a quaint observance takes me 'out of the world,' I am dedicating my life to an illusion."[13] The monastic choice was simultaneously traditional and countercultural. "The monk," he says, "is someone who takes up a critical attitude toward the contemporary world and its structures."[14] While Merton dwelled physically in the cloister of the monastery in Kentucky, his heart was broken and praying for the modernistic deserts of twentieth-century humanity he saw in contemporary city streets and alleyways. The comparison that Merton draws between the desert fathers and mothers and life in the multicultural city is timely—it is a call to remember the time before Christianity was confined by theoretical walls of the religious institution. This call is echoed in many of the conversations and surveys we had with young adults in all regions of the nation. Merton makes clear that "the monastic horizon is clearly the horizon of the desert. The monastic church is the church of the wilderness, the woman who has fled into the desert from the dragon that seeks to devour the infant Word."[15] There is a thirst for something beyond the

---

13. Thomas Merton, "Contemplation in a World of Action," cited in *Thomas Merton: Spiritual Master* (New York, 1992), 376.

14. Merton, *Thomas Merton: Spiritual Master*, 376.

15. Thomas Merton, *The Silent Life* (New York: Farrar, Straus and Giroux, 1999), xiii–xiv.

artifice and deadness that the fossilized trees of religious institutions want to offer young adults, and the thirst is finding new wells to drink from, as you will hear in the chapters that follow.

As seen in his reflections on the desert tradition in *Wisdom of the Desert*, Merton provides a challenge to many rigid forms of Christian spirituality that seek method over encounter and critique without conviction. After decades of tragedies such as Columbine, 9/11, Sandy Hook, the shooting death of Trayvon Martin and on and on, communities of faith continue to reinforce certainty and safety as the baseline for faithfulness in ways that are often counter to the marks of the life of the Spirit. This is not an acceptable pathway for the young adults we have worked with. For Merton, we who live in a spiritual wilderness as did the desert fathers and mothers are called to seek the void that God wishes to fill and not merely avoid the reality of the void within us: "With the Desert Fathers, you have the characteristic of a clean break with a conventional, accepted social context in order to swim for one's life into an apparently irrational void."[16] While a call to deep justice amid the masses of the city is dampened by the loudest voices of election cycles and economic drives for profit at all cost, Merton compels those who live in cities to stand together in the sacred silence of God.

In these times when the ecumenical, racial, and class concerns of the city continue to explode with tension and fear, authentic reconciliation is needed now more than ever. Merton challenges those who live in today's cities not only to pray for mercy and forgiveness, but to actively pray for the ability to love. We are called not to reinforce the proverbial walls that surround and sustain the places where we live but to seek the center point of why we live at all. For the disenfranchised who seek meaning and purpose, Merton writes that that meaning and purpose in the urban world will be grounded neither in the material nor in the dogmatic, but in the life that is lived

16. Thomas Merton, *Wisdom of the Desert* (New York: New Directions, 1960), 9.

with open hands where absence of certainty is embraced rather than feared. Instead of creating stronger walls or systems, our goal should be the patient, persistent turn toward what is at the center of our humanity—even if our cities as we have nostalgically remembered them never return.

This is highlighted in Merton's famous "Letters to a White Liberal" written in 1963 when he prophetically acknowledges what Ta-Nehisi Coates and others underscored decades later: America will continue to struggle with class and race until radical change is allowed to take place and ultimately dismantle the essential form of our current life. As Merton stated in the 1960s:

> The problem is this: if the Negro, as he actually is (not the "ideal" and theoretical Negro, or even the educated and cultured Negro of the small minority), enters wholly into white society, then *that society is going to be radically changed.* This of course is what the White South very well knows, and it is what the white Liberal has failed to understand. Not only will there be a radical change which, whatever form it may take, will amount to at least a peaceful revolution, but also there will be enormous difficulties and sacrifices demanded of everyone, especially the whites.[17]

As Merton foresaw, without the ability to allow for radical change at all levels, change would be limited and therefore never truly be change. In this Merton is essentially putting forward that the very form of our lives must change at a profound level, not merely our ideology or aspirations.

In his 1919 lecture "On the Idea of a Theology of Culture," Paul Tillich argues a similar point by asserting that authentic religious experience is found amid the triadic interplay of content, form, and meaning (*Gehalt*), to which he links the terms "autonomy," "heteronomy,"

17. Thomas Merton, *Seeds of Destruction* (New York: Farrar, Straus & Giroux, 1964), 8; emphasis original.

and "theonomy."[18] Content denotes something objective in its simple existence that represents what we culturally value. The act of giving form to content creates a recognizable structure within the cultural sphere—be it a city street, building, war memorial, or elementary school. Meaning is something else again: it is the depth-meaning, the spiritual substance of a cultural product. In a traditional formulation of Tillich's paradigm, content coupled with meaning is essential for human flourishing, and form mediates between content and meaning. The power of form to mediate and control meaning and content is exemplified in Coates's notion of the Dream that plagues our culture and continually frames race as an antithetical referent to the ideal life:

> I have seen that dream all my life. It is perfect houses with nice lawns. It is Memorial Day cookouts, block associations, and driveways. The Dream is treehouses and the Cub Scouts. The Dream smells like peppermint but tastes like strawberry shortcake. And for so long I wanted to escape into The Dream, to fold my country over my head like a blanket. But this has never been an option because The Dream rests on our backs, the bedding made from our bodies. And knowing this, knowing that The Dream persists by warring with the known world, I was sad for the host, I was sad for all those families, I was sad for my country, but above all, in that moment, I was sad for you.[19]

What Coates so provocatively describes is at the heart of Merton's letter to white liberals and is central to Tillich's point of the controlling nature of form over content and meaning in religion—and it's the lacuna in Murray's *Coming Apart*. Without the prophetic

18. Paul Tillich, "On the Idea of a Theology of Culture" in *What Is Religion?*, trans. James L. Adams (New York: Harper and Row, 1969), 165.
19. Ta-Nehisi Coates, *Between the World and Me* (New York: Spiegel & Grau, 2015), 11.

imagination[20] and courage to let go of our systems and forms entirely and allow the silent void to awaken us to our crippling idolatry in the forms and systems of Coates's notion of the Dream, we will repeat the horrors of history rather than learn from them. In this way we will defend the Dream even if it is built on the bedding of the bodies of young black men shot in the streets again and again. This monastic critique leveled by Merton and picked up by Coates is always a perpetual self-critique as well, one that leads to an abiding conviction and love for the other.

As seen throughout Merton's writings, the true monastic individual knows that the chaos of the world is no more than a macrocosm in his or her own soul. A person who envisions the monastic choice as a decision to retreat from the world is someone who has failed. The monastic choice for Merton is one of conviction and critique. It is not a protest against the world *per se*, only against the world's limited thinking that dismisses the ultimate concerns of the body and soul. It is the choice to be liberated from the confines of human potentiality that the world wants us to believe in. As he writes in "A Letter on the Contemplative Life":

> It is true that when I came to the monastery where I am I came in revolt against the meaningless confusion of a life in which there was so much activity, so much movement, so much useless talk . . . that I could not remember who I was. But the fact remains that my flight from the world is not a reproach to you who remain in the world, and I have no right to repudiate the world in a purely negative fashion, because if I do that my flight will have not taken me to truth and to God but to a private, though doubtless, pious illusion.[21]

20. Walter Brueggemann, *The Prophetic Imagination*, 2nd ed. (Minneapolis: Fortress, 2001).
21. Merton, *Thomas Merton: Spiritual Master*, 424.

In seeking after a renewed sense of deep faith within the multicultural city that young adults call home in the postpandemic twenty-first century, the challenge of Merton's vision is to reclaim the call for what I have named previously a "monasticism without walls" within our contemporary discussions of urban renewal, the future of just institutions such as Christian higher education and the church, and the attentive ear to listen for the prophetic in the midst of the banal.

Conjectures of a Guilty Bystander, arguably Merton's best-known contribution to political activism, stated that true monasticism is a political and spiritual protest—a notion also reflected in the actions and passions of the young adults we have worked with over the years, both pre- and postpandemic.[22] It is the protest of the humble and the contrite as opposed to the protest of the sanctimonious and the righteous. It is a deeper and more hazardous kind of protest than we see often televised. It begins by dwelling not on the evils of the world but on the failure of the self to love and find love in God instead of in the culture that beckons us like a siren to the rocks. "[The monastic] flight is not an evasion. If the monk were able to understand what goes on inside him, he would be able to say how well he knows that the battle [of the world] is being fought in his own heart."[23] Therefore retreat is not always abandonment; it is sometimes deep critique, especially when we retreat more deeply into and not away from the center of the storm.

Although the desert fathers and mothers were deeply influential for Merton, he was acutely aware of the dangers of reviving their asceticism in our modern society, knowing that God had to become more a part of our world, not less. He also knew that the model of retreat, which was the conventional way modern people viewed monasticism, was not a productive one for the twentieth century. As seen in the chapters that follow, the work of listening to and learning

22. Thomas Merton, *Conjectures of a Guilty Bystander* (Garden City, NY: Image Books, 1966).
23. Merton, *The Silent Life*, xiv.

from young adults will require much, much more than mere reflection without action.

Faithful Space as Reclaiming Church as "Church"

While it may seem counterintuitive, one path forward in working with young adults is a reclaiming of religiosity for the sake of community. Though the word "religiosity" is often used in current parlance to indicate narrow-mindedness, the Jewish philosopher Martin Buber uses it in a different way. He writes that "religiosity induces sons, who want to find their own God, to rebel against their fathers; religion induces fathers to reject their sons, who will not let their father's God be forced upon them. *Religion means preservation; religiosity, renewal.*"[24] As a mystic of sorts, Buber sees religiosity as a spiritual movement that claims both tradition and the current moment—hand in hand—for the sake of reconciliation. Where religion bends toward the static moment, religiosity strives for dynamic movement. In a similar fashion, Merton believed that what we need is not more religion but more religiosity—what Martin Buber calls "the elemental entering-into-relation with the Absolute,"[25] which is counter to the "nostalgia for the absolute" that Steiner fears. Merton recognized that we need to reconnect to the roots of the true spiritual quest prior to any attempts at solving the urban blight and malaise of our time; those roots had become fossilized in formalized institutional religion, beginning in the fourth century for Merton and the rabbinic period (second century) for Buber. Both Buber and Merton knew the extent to which this pursuit of religiosity demanded rebellion, not against the secular state but against the very institutions of religion.

24. Martin Buber, "Jewish Religiosity," in *On Judaism: An Introduction to the Essence of Judaism by One of the Most Important Religious Thinkers of the Twentieth Century* (New York: Schocken, 1967), 80–81.
25. Buber, "Jewish Religiosity," 80.

Faithful Space as Traditionality not Traditionalism

For Merton, renewal meant retrieving the past by questioning the "tra ditional" presentation of it. He desired traditionality and not traditionalism. Yale historian Jaroslav Pelikan suggests the following distinction between "tradition" and "traditionalism": "tradition is the 'living faith of the dead,' traditionalism is 'the dead faith of the living.'"[26] Traditionality, in accord with Merton's idea of renewal, continually holds counsel with the dead and makes religiosity in modernity "the living faith of the living." By living deeply in tradition, yet also on its margins, one can revive the religiosity dormant within it. To do that, however, requires a protest against tradition itself, whose fatal flaw is that its adherents seek to preserve the past—akin to Coates's Dream—even at the expense of the creativity of the present. Traditions perpetuate themselves by trying to ward off, or at least to control, change. This is akin to feeding on mineralized watersheds rather than seeking deeper wells. Traditionality, which is founded on perpetual critique, does not seek to perpetuate itself. Its success creates its own obsolescence. Merton believed that commitment to tradition, even in its corrupt form, could lead to the desert, which he envisioned as the "living faith of the living." It is alive precisely because it is unstable, precarious, and unpredictable. To live a dead faith is to live solely in the institution of religion, and this is similar to embracing the essentialism of the past form of cities as described by Murray and Putnam, who lament its loss. Merton constantly tried to diffuse the romantic and sentimentalist notion of the monastic life, maintaining that romanticism too often leads to nostalgia, which has no place in the authentic monastic quest. Traditionality is lived by embracing tradition while simultaneously moving beyond it. In doing so, Merton believed, its essence is liberated and revived. In this sense, Merton knew the power of obedience and its indispensability to evoke love:

26. Jaroslav Pelikan, *The Vindication of Tradition: The 1983 Jefferson Lectures on the Humanities* (New Haven, CT: Yale University Press, 1986), 62.

The higher and more perfect union of wills in love (the goal of the monk) will not be possible if the lower and more elemental union of wills in obedience is lacking. It is an error to appeal to love against obedience. But it is also an error to reduce all love in practice to obedience alone, as if the two were synonymous. Love is much deeper than obedience, but unless obedience opens up all those inner spiritual depths our love will remain superficial, a matter of sentiment and emotion, little more.[27]

By embracing a call for monastic activism, Merton entered a vocation modernity scorned, while remaining a vital part of the modern project and offering those of us in the era of "coming apart" another element to consider in rebuilding our world. As we consider the analyses of Murray and Putnam in conversation with the critiques and convictions of Merton, Buber, and Coates, our vocation is to move further into our diverse communities at their deepest levels. There faith, hope, and love, rather than merely rebuilding the Dream in crisis, hopefully listen and respond to the God in whom we live and move and have our being.

Several themes arise once we enter a truly faithful space, and over the five years of our work with congregations and faith communities, we have identified some of the most distinctive and essential of those themes. In the following chapters we will hear from several researchers on the Pivot NW Research team who have been a part of this work and many who are young adults themselves. In their wanderings through the various communities and their deep analytical and pastoral reflections, they have brought new hope and new life to how we should understand what it means to be faithful in all our spaces of life, whether those are work, family, or in sacred space.

In "Emerging Faithfulness: Young Adulthood in the Twenty-First Century," we expand on the growing sociological and theological

---

27. Thomas Merton, *Life and Holiness* (New York: Herder & Herder, 1963), 43–44.

literature that sees the developmental markers for young adults shifting in our culture today. Highlighting the work of Jeffrey Arnett and Melinda Denton on emerging adulthood, we set the table for how we can better prepare a space for faithfulness that is hospitable to young adults.

In "Young Adults and Religious Affiliation: Research and Reflections," Gabrielle Metzler and Mathea Kangas, two industrial and organizational psychologists—and young adults themselves—underscore the importance to young adults of the search for faithfulness and faithful spaces by centering on the question of how religious affiliation shapes what young adults look for as they enter spaces of work and life. They offer some current quantitative research we did both regionally and nationally that asked young adults what on-ramps and off-ramps they see when entering spaces of faith and work, as well as what markers for growth and development they seek.

In "Deep Listening and Young Adults: Thematic Analysis," Lauren St. Martin, a graduate of Fuller Theological Seminary and Church Communications and Ethnographic Lead at Pivot NW Research, moves the conversation from quantitative data to more qualitative data collection based on the many hours our Pivot NW Research team spent sitting and listening to young adults in various settings: homes, church basements, places of work, places of recreation and play. These conversations—thematic analysis—were all recorded and coded to find major themes embedded in the stories of how young adults made sense of their longings and hopes for faithful spaces. This thematic analysis work brought together some important themes that faithful spaces should be attentive to.

In "Church as Resource Station: Young Adults in Transition," Linda Montaño, an industrial and organizational psychologist on the Pivot NW Research team, gathered the data and conversations we collected and centered on how churches today that seek to be faithful spaces for young adults could begin to reimagine themselves as "resource stations"—places where young adults in transition can come and dwell with mentors and other young adults without the pressure of an indefinite commitment of time. In this way, Montaño picks up on how emerging adulthood as seen in the earlier chapters is always about movement and growth rather than staying put and finishing growth. This chapter offers some encouragement to churches that already have resources to offer as faithful spaces and suggestions on how to make a renewed commitment to caring for young adults in transition.

In "Identified Not Developed: Young Adults in Leadership" Mackenzie Harris, an industrial and organizational psychologist on the Pivot NW Research team, expands on the role that churches can and should play as resource stations for young adults in transition by offering a call to churches to see young adults as leaders fully realized when they come and dwell in faithful spaces. Where some leadership models have focused on leadership as "development"—creating barriers and rungs on a ladder for young adults to climb prior to being allowed leadership roles—Harris is instead arguing that churches move to leadership as "identification" by advocating for the on-ramping of young adults into leadership once they come into the community. In this way, young adults should be involved in power sharing and reciprocal mentorship in which faithful spaces adjust their expectations upward and expect more, not less, from young adults, which will in turn build commitment and trust.

In "Young Adults and New Church Models" Martin Jiménez, Project Manager for Pivot NW Research and a graduate of Fuller Seminary and ruling elder in the Presbyterian Church (USA), looks at the history and possibilities of faithful spaces in relation to new church developments. As Jiménez reflects on the question "What form should and will the church of tomorrow take?" he accounts for the reality that churches of today are building on and overturning prior church growth systems. Akin to fallen trees in the forest that become nurse logs that provide the base nutrients for new growth, old church models can provide strength, but also stagnate and stifle new growth and imagination for future faithful spaces. This chapter provides both cautionary tales as well as prophetic commissioning for how the form of faithful spaces should develop.

In "Conclusion: Active Love and the Hope of Communities of Loving Defiance," I return to one of the dominant themes identified from our research with young adults: the reality of economic uncertainty and the role that economics plays in the faith development of young adults. Here I argue for a more holistic view of economics whereby faithful communities seek to address the fullness of young adults' development in mind, body, and spirit and see in this a call to support economic health and wellness. As seen in the cultural move from postmodernity to our current reality of metamodernism, young adults are seeking life-work balance in all aspects of their life, and that includes how they engage with faithful spaces. In this regard there is a lot to relearn for churches and workplaces from the prophetic literature of the Old Testament on the topic of Jubilee, as well as on how the calls to justice and righteousness in all aspects of life are essential for young adults seeking to deepen and grow faith.

1

Emerging Faithfulness

Young Adulthood in the Twenty-First Century

JEFFREY F. KEUSS AND ROBERT DROVDAHL

It's out of your hands, but have a safe flight
My thoughts, all noise, fake smile, decoys
Sometimes, I need to hear your voice.

—boygenius, "Black Hole"

Emerging adulthood cannot be comprehended apart from an understanding of adolescence as a separate stage in the life cycle. At the dawn of the twentieth century, G. Stanley Hall's seminal work on the teen years solidified in Western culture a new recognition of this period in the human life cycle—adolescence.[1] Midway through the twentieth century, Erik Erikson designated adolescence as one of

---

An earlier version of this chapter appeared as "Emerging Adults and Christian Faith: The Faith Experience of Emerging Adults in the Pacific Northwest," *Christian Education Journal Research on Education Ministry* 17 (April 2020). Reprinted by permission of SAGE Publications.

1. G. Stanley Hall, *Adolescence: Its Psychology and Its Relations to*

eight stages in the life cycle, sandwiched between later childhood and early adulthood.[2] The social context of awareness of this stage was and is industrialized society, where becoming an adult is a *transitional experience* more than an *event*. As a result, adulthood is chronologically delayed, due largely to the extended education needed to ready oneself for the roles and responsibilities of adult life.

Since its publication in 1950, Erik Erikson's theory of psychosocial development has guided understanding of human growth across the life cycle, particularly in Western, industrialized societies. Now, at the dawn of the twenty-first century, theorists are proposing a new stage in the human life cycle. Rooted chiefly in the research of Jeffrey Arnett, emerging adulthood seems to be the moniker that has stuck for this newly acknowledged stage between adolescence and young adulthood.[3] This chapter chronicles the rise of emerging adulthood as a distinct developmental stage; identifies general, research-based descriptions of emerging adults; documents the findings of a Lilly Endowment funded research project on the faith of emerging adults; and, finally, proposes ministry implications in light of the findings.

Research Support for Emerging Adulthood

What reality lies behind the moniker? Arnett argues for both an internal and external reality, insisting that emerging adulthood is truly a psychosocial stage in the life span. While there has not been a single, precise social marker of the transition to adulthood in Western industrialized societies, there has been a set of external conditions typically associated with moving into the full measure of adulthood. People are taking longer to pass these markers, thus creating the social conditions for a new life stage. Deferred marriage is often seen

Physiology, Anthropology, Sociology, Sex, Crime, Religion and Education (New York: Appleton, 1904).

2. Erik Erikson, *Childhood and Society* (New York: Norton, 1950).

3. Jeffrey J. Arnett, *Emerging Adulthood: The Winding Road from the Late Teens through the Twenties* (New York: Oxford University Press, 2014).

as the most prominent form of delayed entry into adulthood. When Erikson wrote *Childhood and Society* in 1950, the median age of first marriage for women was just over twenty years old; the median age for men was just under twenty-three years old.[4] According to the most recent US Census data, the median age of marriage in 2022 is nearly twenty-eight years of age for women and nearly thirty years of age for men.[5] Clearly, marriage was much closer chronologically to the end of adolescence in 1950 than in 2022.

A second external marker of fully transitioning to adulthood has been completing education and entering the workforce. Again, a remarkable shift has occurred on this front. In 1950 approximately 25 percent of people aged eighteen through twenty-four had some college-level education and only 6 percent of people twenty-five years of age and up had a college degree. By 2016, nearly 34 percent of people aged twenty-five and up had completed a college degree.[6]

A third external marker of a fully transitioned adult is relative stability in terms of "place," both geographic location and work environment. The extended time needed to "settle down" partly defines emerging adulthood. As Smith notes, emerging adulthood is a distinctive phase due to the fact that "changes in the American and global economy undermine stable, lifelong careers and replace them with careers with lower job security, more frequent job changes and an ongoing need for new training and education."[7] Arnett cites

4. Jeffrey J. Arnett, *Emerging Adults in America: Coming of Age in the Twenty-First Century* (Washington, DC: American Psychological Association, 2008).

5. "Figure MS-2 Median Age at First Marriage: 1890 to Present," U.S. Census Bureau, 2022, https://www.census.gov/content/dam/Census/li brary/visualizations/time-series/demo/families-and-households/ms-2.pdf.

6. "Highest Educational Attainment Levels since 1940," U.S. Census Bureau, https://www.census.gov/library/visualizations/2017/comm/cb17-51 _educational_attainment.html.

7. Christian Smith, Kari Christoffersen, Hilary Davidson, and Patricia S. Herzog, *Lost in Transition: The Dark Side of Emerging Adulthood* (Oxford: Oxford University Press, 2011), 14.

US Census data showing the highest percentage of Americans who changed residences were people in the twenty-to-twenty-four-year age bracket.[8] Over one-third of people in this age bracket had changed residences based on 2002 data.

A fourth external marker of a fully transitioned adult is financial independence. Here again, launching children into adulthood requires extended parental financial support. Smith cites a study showing that parents contributed, on average, nearly $40,000 in material support to each of their children *after* the child turned eighteen.[9] If financial independence is a characteristic of adult life, a significant number of people aged eighteen to thirty are still dependent on family economic support during these years and hence have not fully entered adulthood.

Of course, these factors interconnect and additional external markers could be identified, but the point is clear: significant changes in the shape and structure of society have changed the shape and structure of the life cycle as well as people's sense of identity as they move through it.

Five Features of Emerging Adulthood

While many have offered descriptions of the psychological dimensions of this stage, Arnett's work has provided the most research-grounded picture of emerging adults. Arnett identifies five psychodynamic features which describe how people in this period of life perceive and experience their lives.[10] Here are brief descriptions of the five features.

First, emerging adults engage in *identity exploration*, particularly in reference to work and love relationships. Of course, identity formation is a key task of adolescence as well, so one might ask how the work of identity formation differs in the two stages. Arnett suggests the key distinction is a more long-term perspective among emerging

8. Arnett, *Emerging Adulthood.*
9. Smith et al., *Lost in Transition.*
10. Arnett, *Emerging Adults in America.*

adults for both work and love relationships. For example, adolescents might ask themselves whether they enjoy their job, while emerging adults are more likely to ask whether their work will be a sustainable source of satisfaction. Adolescents typically do not link their identity to the jobs they hold or see connection between successive jobs; emerging adults seek jobs that can be stepping stones to long-term careers and are more closely connected to their identities.

Second, emerging adults see their lives as marked by *instability*. This quality matches the external conditions of society. When seen positively, emerging adults will see this time as the opportunity and freedom to explore and try new ways of existing in the world, without being tied down with long-term commitments to work, relationships, or responsibilities. Seen negatively, this condition reflects something akin to wandering in the wilderness, with no way out.[11]

Third, emerging adults are *self-focused*. Just as egocentrism should not be equated with egotism, neither should self-focus be equated with selfishness. Generally speaking, emerging adults' relative freedom for agency and their freedom from obligations in relationships provide a context for self-focus. While there are constraints, many emerging adults are "on their own" in making life choices, whether those choices have minimal or significant consequences. Emerging adults' relationships also provide more flexibility, with fewer sustained obligations that impinge on their time and resources.

Fourth, emerging adults feel *in-between*. One research question Arnett regularly asked subjects in this age range was, "Do you feel that you have reached adulthood?"[12] Nearly 60 percent of his subjects (age eighteen to twenty-five) answered this question "yes and no." Virtually none of his subjects thought of themselves as adolescents, while approximately 40 percent thought they had reached adulthood.

11. Brian Simmons, *Wandering in the Wilderness: Changes and Challenges to Emerging Adults' Christian Faith* (Abilene, TX: Abilene Christian University Press, 2011).

12. Arnett, *Emerging Adults in America*, 303–30.

These perceptions varied substantially from subjects aged twelve to seventeen and subjects aged twenty-six to thirty-five. Again, this inner psychological identity mirrors well a culture without a clear picture of when one becomes an adult.

Finally, emerging adults see the *possibilities* in this stage of life. Emerging adults are remarkably hopeful about their lives. In that sense, emerging adults typically believe in the *American Dream*; they believe their lives will turn out as they hope, with meaningful work, healthy relationships, and a satisfying trajectory. Emerging adults possess the quality Daniel Levinson described as "the dream," that idealistic hope that propels a person into the adult years.[13]

Educational Ministry and Developmental Theory

As mentioned earlier, Christian researchers have long been interested in the connection between Christian faith formation and human development. Much of this engagement came before emerging adulthood began to be recognized as a distinct stage. For example, Les Steele has explored broad parallels between developmental theory and faith formation. In part four of *On the Way: A Practical Theology of Christian Formation*, Steele examines cycles of Christian formation in each of Erikson's eight life-cycle stages.[14] Others focus on more particular interactions. In *Religious Thinking from Childhood to Adolescence*, Goldman studied how children in Jean Piaget's concrete operations stage understood and interpreted biblical stories.[15] Drawing on Lawrence Kohlberg's theory of moral development,[16] many Christian educators have examined how a person's moral reasoning might affect a biblical

13. Daniel J. Levinson, *The Seasons of Man's Life* (New York: Knopf, 1978).

14. Les L. Steele, *On the Way: A Practical Theology of Christian Formation* (Grand Rapids: Baker, 1990).

15. Ronald Goldman, *Religious Thinking from Childhood to Adolescence* (New York: Seabury, 1968).

16. Lawrence Kohlberg, "Stages of Moral Development as a Basis for Moral Education," *Harvard Educational Review* 34, no. 1 (1964): 1–23.

understanding of justice.[17] Of course, the quintessential work on connecting faith formation and human development likely is that of James
Fowler. Following in Kohlberg's footsteps, Fowler used structural developmental theory to construct a model of faith formation across
the life span. Based on 359 interviews conducted between 1972 and
1981, Fowler proposed a six-stage, hierarchically integrated sequence
of faith development in his seminal work, *Stages of Faith*.[18] Each stage
represented a distinctive way of holding and experiencing faith.

While general work has been done on human development and
Christian formation, research is needed on particular interactions
between Christian formation and emerging adulthood. One can find
good work on ministry implications focused on a research-based picture of emerging adulthood. For example, David Setran and Chris
Kiesling have published a comprehensive volume that considers how
one might work theologically with themes such as church, vocation,
sexuality, and morality in light of emerging adulthood.[19] In *Wandering in the Wilderness*, Brian Simmons explores the ways emerging
adulthood affects one's perspective on Christian faith, participation
in church, relational life, and faith practices.[20] Simmons blends general research on emerging adults with stories gathered in his role as
a university professor and church pastor.

While this chapter will conclude with ministry implications, its focus is not on ministry application. It is rather on describing a research
project that aims to learn how being an emerging adult shapes one's

17. Michael J. Anthony, *Introducing Christian Education: Foundations for
the Twenty-First Century* (Grand Rapids: Baker Academic, 2001); Robert W.
Pazmiño, *Foundational Issues in Christian Education: An Introduction in Evangelical Perspective* (Grand Rapids: Baker, 1988).

18. James W. Fowler, *Stages of Faith: The Psychology of Human Development and the Quest for Meaning* (New York: HarperOne, 1995).

19. David P. Setran, *Spiritual Formation in Emerging Adulthood: A Practical Theology for College and Young Adult Ministry* (Grand Rapids: Baker
Academic, 2013).

20. Simmons, *Wandering in the Wilderness*.

experience of Christian faith. The research is one component of a grant program, Pivot Northwest, funded by the Lilly Endowment. Understanding emerging adults' experience of faith is crucial for ministry with this group, since that experience affects their identity and their perceptions of Christianity. An analogue for this focus is Michael Emerson and Christian Smith's study of racialization as a characteristic of American society, so a brief description of their research will be helpful.[21]

In *Divided by Faith*, a study of evangelical Protestant faith and race in America, Emerson and Smith employ the concept of "racialized society" to describe differences in how people experience life in America as a result of their race. For Emerson and Smith, a racialized society is "a society where race matters profoundly for differences in life experiences, life opportunities, and social relationships."[22] "Racialization" as the entry point for examining the relationship between evangelicals and race provides an advantage over terms such as "racist" or "racism" for at least three reasons:

- It focuses more on *description* than evaluation, thus minimizing judgmentalism.
- It focuses on people's *present experience*, rather than causation and blame.
- It focuses on the *intersection of a significant identity marker and lived experience, without* drawing conclusions about character.

Our research works in a similar manner with emerging adults and faith. We believe that developmental eras matter profoundly for differences in the way humans experience faith. We are interested in how being an emerging adult shapes the experience of Christian faith. The particular aspect of Christian faith under review is faithful-

---

21. Michael O. Emerson and Christian Smith, *Divided by Faith: Evangelical Religion and the Problem of Race in America* (Oxford: Oxford University Press, 2001).
22. Emerson and Smith, *Divided by Faith*, 7.

ness. The question driving the Pivot NW Research project is: How do emerging adult Christians perceive faithfulness? Jesus ends his parable of the persistent widow with a question: "And yet, when the Son of Man comes, will he find faith on earth?" (Luke 18:8). The Pivot NW Research study attempts to describe the faith Jesus might find among emerging adults in the first quarter of the twenty-first century.

Emerging Adults in the Pacific Northwest

The largest age demographic in the Pacific Northwest is twenty-to-twenty-nine-year-olds, who represent 22 percent of the region's population. Although nearly one-third of the region's adults self-identify as Christian,[23] most Pacific Northwesterners do not belong to a church, synagogue, temple, or mosque, and it has been this way for over one hundred years. In 2000, 62.8 percent of adults in the Pacific Northwest considered themselves "outside" of religious communities. Fewer Pacific Northwest adults are church *adherents* than in any other region of the country. Adherents comprised only 37.2 percent of the total population, including children, in the Pacific Northwest in 2000 compared to the national figure of 59.5 percent. Those who are in religious organizations are divided and dispersed amongst more distinct and diverse religious bodies than is the case in other regions of the United States. The top five Christian traditions in other parts of the United States (Roman Catholic, Methodist, Baptist, Pentecostal/Charismatic, and Reformed) capture 75 percent to 80 percent of the adherents nationwide. Hence these top five groups found in other regions of the United States dominate the "religious marketplace" in those places and therefore provide the context and grammar by which individuals and communities discuss and understand matters of faith.

In the Pacific Northwest, however, the top five groups in the re-

---

23. "Statistical Abstract of the United States: 2021," US Census Bureau, https://www.census.gov/library/publications/2011/compendia/statab /131ed.html.

gion capture only 66 percent of adherents. Given that the total "pie" of adherents is so small in this region, it makes it difficult for any single denomination to exert significant social or political influence. For example, Roman Catholics, the largest group in the Pacific Northwest, accounted for only 11.3 percent of the population in 2000. Patricia Killen, lead researcher and author of *Religion and Public Life in the Pacific Northwest: The None Zone* underscores this point during an interview with Matthew Kaemingk:

> The Pacific Northwest lacks a dominant religious community alongside or over against which individuals and communities construct their religious identities. In much of the South you are Baptist or working at not being a Baptist. In Minnesota over 50% of the population, when *The None Zone* was written, were Lutheran or Catholic. In the Pacific Northwest the single largest religious body is the Roman Catholic Church, which is only 11.3% of the population. That is a significantly smaller percentage than the 25% who responded "none" when asked, "What is your religious affiliation, if any?"[24]

Given these findings, demographically it is small wonder that many churches in the region have had difficulty finding a form and grammar for faith that is conversant with Pacific Northwest culture.

Emerging Adults Seek Connection, Not Conversion

As seen in the following chapters, the ability to see, hear, touch, and feel the embodied reality of communal spiritual commitment is a necessity for emerging adults to find authenticity. Recent studies of emerging adult spirituality show that a key indicator of sustained re-

---

24. Matthew Kaemingk, "Pacific Northwest Religion: Doing It Different, Doing It Alone," *Christ & Cascadia*, October 25, 2013, https://christandcascadia.com/2013/10/25/religion-in-the-pacific-northwest-doing-it-different/.

lationships within a faith community is found when a community ultimately fosters a generative relationship with God as an interactive bond between a person and God.

The term "interactive bond" is used by sociologists of religion to underscore a necessary shift in perception away from trends that limit the event horizon of faith communities primarily to events and programs that allow for anonymity or to social media. To the contrary, deep and abiding communities for emerging adults are found and forged within relationships of presence and purpose navigating the following relational dimensions:[25] (1) *intimacy*, in which the interactive bond between person and God is experienced as close and warm; (2) *consistency*, in which the interactive bond between person and God is experienced as steady and predictable; (3) *anxiety*, in which both internal and external challenges to the interactive bond between person and God found in worry and uncertainty are named and dealt with; and (4) *anger*, in which failed expectations relating to the interactive bond between person and God resulting in feelings of hostility can be worked on toward holistic healing and reconciliation.

Emerging Adults Seek Personal Well-Being

This call to forge and sustain authentic interactive bonds between persons and God has been acknowledged and taken up even in communities that are distinctly nonreligious. These attract many emerging adults called "spiritual but not religious" (SBNR) in Linda Mercadante's 2014 qualitative study *Belief without Borders: Inside the Minds of the Spiritual but Not Religious*.[26] Mercadante's study of SBNR adults found five typologies among those self-reporting as SBNR:

---

25. Nicolette Manglos-Weber, "Relationships with God among Young Adults: Validating a Measurement Model with Four Dimensions," *Sociology of Religion* 77, no. 2 (2016).

26. Linda A. Mercadante, *Belief without Borders: Inside the Minds of the Spiritual but Not Religious* (New York: Oxford University Press, 2014).

(1) dissenters, (2) casuals, (3) explorers, (4) seekers, and (5) immigrants. Those who were twenty to twenty-nine largely self-reported (half of all millennials in her study) typologically as casuals, for whom "spiritual practices are used primarily as a way toward better health, stress relief, or emotional support." This is, thus, a "therapeutic spirituality focused on personal well-being."[27] This is supported in the recent Harvard Divinity School-Crestwood Foundation qualitative research study entitled "How We Gather,"[28] in which six distinctive themes arose that were seen as emblematic of thriving organizations serving young adults in nonreligious contexts:

- *Community*: valuing and fostering deep relationships that center on service to others
- *Personal transformation*: making a conscious and dedicated effort to develop one's own body, mind, and spirit
- *Social transformation*: pursuing justice and beauty in the world through the creation of networks for good
- *Purpose finding*: clarifying, articulating, and acting on one's personal mission in life
- *Creativity*: allowing time and space to activate the imagination and engage in play
- *Accountability*: holding oneself and others responsible for working toward defined goals

What is clear in the research of twenty-to-twenty-nine-year-old emerging adults in the Pacific Northwest is that the desire to gather, spiritually grow, be intellectually challenged, seek holistic healing, and find deep purpose in life is highly valued, as are communities

27. Mercadante, *Belief without Borders*, 56.
28. Angie Thurston and Casper ter Kuile, "How We Gather: The Rise of Unaffiliated Millennials," Harvard Divinity School and Crestwood Foundation report, 2015, https://caspertk.files.wordpress.com/2015/04/how-we-ga ther1.pdf.

that offer authentic commitments to such emphases. Yet while the research makes this clear, church communities have continued to use the language of "attraction" rather than responsiveness to the clear and present needs of this demographic. Many church communities work on trying to attract twentysomethings into existing systems that are offered as legacy rather than true community. Such attempts can make the church come across as an immutable antique rather than a generative relationship where all parties grow and change through intimacy and trust. The issue for many church communities in the Pacific Northwest is not a lack of twenty-to-twenty-nine-year-olds in the population seeking community and spiritual nourishment. Rather, the issue is whether church communities understand the emerging adults who populate the Pacific Northwest and are sufficiently equipped to create a hospitable space for them.

The Pivot NW Research Study

In the fall of 2016, Seattle Pacific University's School of Theology received an initial $1.5 million grant from the Lilly Endowment to help congregations in the Pacific Northwest engage emerging adults, working with them to design innovative ministries that support and enrich their faith lives. This grant was one component of the Lilly Endowment's nationwide "Young Adult Initiative," aimed at helping congregations design and launch new ministries with emerging adults, ages twenty-three to twenty-nine. Grants were made to twelve colleges, universities, and seminaries in ten states and the District of Columbia to establish innovation hubs to serve these congregations.

The five-year project's early task was to identify faith communities to work with, helping them better understand the experiences of emerging adults and working with them to design, launch, and evaluate new ministries. Included in this work was research on emerging adults' experience of faith. In 2017–2018, Pivot NW Research surveyed twenty-three-to-twenty-nine-year-old adults to better understand their needs and concerns regarding Christianity and Christian faith communities. Each survey focused on one of the three primary research questions:

- Why do emerging adults attend or not attend church?
- What distinctive contributions does church make to the lives of emerging adults?
- How do emerging adults grow in faith through engagement with church?

The results of these research questions will be discussed in the following chapter.

Central to concerns of emerging adulthood as a paradigm are the state of faith communities and faith community participation. Census data has shown an almost uniform decline in emerging adult participation in faith communities over the past few decades. While religiosity may not mean regular church attendance, faith is still important to many emerging adults. This has been addressed most directly through the research efforts of the National Study of Youth and Religion (NSYR). Adolescent church attendance decreases with age.[29] Within the emerging adult stage of Christian faith development, there is diversity in how emerging adults approach faith growth and religious commitment.

Given the diversity found in adolescent faith growth and religious commitment, it is expected that these emerging adults might continue to differ from each other. In particular, using latent class analysis has shown that with diversity in economic, racial, and cultural contexts comes diversity of developmental concerns.[30] Also, emerging adults in different latent classes experience differences in religiosity after a family breakup and other disruptive trauma.[31] As we approached

29. Lisa Pearce, Jessica Hardie, and Melinda Lundquist Denton, "The Dynamics and Correlates of Religious Service Attendance in Adolescence," *Youth & Society* 48, no. 2 (2013).

30. Pearce, Hardie, and Denton, "The Dynamics and Correlates of Religious Service Attendance in Adolescence," 151–75.

31. Lisa Pearce and Melinda Lundquist Denton, "A Faith of Their Own:

our survey work, we took note of these factors, acknowledging the particularity of our study. Yet in working with other data sets, we find significance that is relatable toward more general application.

Implications for Ministry

Underwriting this project is the question Jesus asked: "And yet, when the Son of Man comes, will he find faith on earth?" We conclude that Jesus would find faith among emerging adults, though the pattern and form of faith will be distinctive to this particular stage in the life cycle. Churches and organizations that seek to serve emerging adults must pay attention to how emerging adults experience Christianity and minister in light of the pattern of faith. We close by highlighting three questions your church or organization might consider as you seek to welcome emerging adults:

Do emerging adults perceive your church or organization as a genuine community with which they can connect? Emerging adults in our study place emphasis on community connection that is reflected in the now familiar sequence, "belong, believe, behave." Belonging is the doorway to faith for emerging adults. Ministry need not focus on relevance (Come because we use the latest technology!), program (Come because we offer big events!), or legacy (Come because you should!). Ministry must focus on creating connections with others that enhance a sense of belonging.

Do emerging adults perceive their encounter with your church or organization as enhancing their well-being? It may be tempting to consider this question as somewhat self-centered, but recall that well-being for emerging adults includes *social transformation, purpose finding,* and *personal transformation.* Emerging adults definitely ask how faith benefits their lives, but they are not simply seeking

---

Stability and Change in the Religiosity of America's Adolescents," *Contemporary Sociology* 31, no. 3 (2012): 356–58.

selfish gain. Ministry must focus on the way in which joining benefits emerging adults' lives.

Do emerging adults perceive your church or organization as offering practices that build a sustainable faith? In this sense, emerging adults are adults! They have a clear sense of what practices help (and do not help) them grow in faith. Churches and Christian organizations cannot simply assume the role of "We know what is good for you." Ministry must invite emerging adults into faith practices that are faith-sustaining so that, indeed, Jesus will find faith among those who occupy this significant stage in the life cycle.

Chapter Reflection Questions

- What is your memory of a stage of life that defined your sense of self? In what ways has this stage of life reminded you of some of the stages found in emergent adulthood discussed in the chapter?
- The chapter talked about the importance of generational mentors—people in your life who offered wisdom and confidence for the person you are becoming. What are some of the characteristics you value and hope for in a mentor?
- What are some of the markers you use for defining when someone is an adult as opposed to a young person? Are some of those markers similar to what is described as emergent adulthood? If they are different, how so?

2

Young Adults and Religious Affiliation

Research and Reflections

GABRIELLE METZLER AND MATHEA KANGAS

Few people enter emerging adulthood at age 18 with a well-established world view, but few people leave their twenties without one, just as few people leave their twenties without a definite direction in love and work.

—Jeffrey J. Arnett[1]

These are the years when it will be easiest to start the lives we want. And no matter what we do, the twenties are an inflection point—the great reorganization—a time when the experiences we have disproportionately influence the adult lives we will lead.

—Meg Jay[2]

1. *Emerging Adulthood: The Winding Road from the Late Teens through the Twenties* (New York: Oxford University Press, 2014), 212.
2. *The Defining Decade: Why Your Twenties Matter and How to Make the Most of Them Now* (New York: Twelve, 2012), 20.

At the beginning of our time with Pivot Northwest, many on our team were just entering young adulthood. Throughout the course of this grant, our research team transitioned from confused, fresh-out-of-college graduate students to employed, married, stable adults. During this journey, we were finding out what we valued; which communities, including the church, could support us in those values; and where we could find our identities, particularly in relation to religion. Part of why we are so excited about this topic is because we have lived it.

While the two of us have had similar experiences as young adults, those in our circle of friends have taken a variety of approaches to this stage of life in both religion and life choices. We both went to graduate school directly from college, married in our mid-twenties, and remain connected to (although not actively involved in) Christianity. Mathea's sister, on the other hand, got married in her early twenties to a man she met at her Christian college, pursued a career as a jeweler, and attends her church Bible study each week. Now she's reduced her work hours and is preparing to become a mother. On the other end of the spectrum, a friend of ours who grew up in the church has moved away from Christianity entirely since leaving home. He's in the process of determining his adult identity, including his career path and significant relationships. One thing he's sure of, though, is that his experience with religion was painful and not something he's going to continue. Yet another young adult we know grew up in a Christian family and has retained her Christian practices, values, and beliefs. As she has started her career and gotten involved in romantic relationships, her faith has been at the center of her decisions. These people constitute a small and relatively homogenous sample of the broader young adult population, coming from similar religious, cultural, and socioeconomic backgrounds. Even so, they showcase the diversity in young adults' approaches to life and faith.

Before we talk about the values, roles, communities, and faith approaches of young adults, let's take a step back. Who are young adults? The term "young adults" refers to twenty-three-to-twenty-nine-year-olds, also referred to as twentysomethings. This group consists of people who are still navigating the challenges of emerging adulthood (a stage that is neither fully adolescent nor fully adult) as well as people who have recently transitioned out of emerging adulthood and are settling into their identities. In the last five to ten years, this age group has been predominantly composed of individuals in the millennial generation.

As noted in the previous chapter, the concept of emerging adulthood is a relatively new phenomenon in the social sciences and has proven to be important as a category in our work. It is during this nebulous but poignant stage of development that individuals navigate numerous identity choices, with few standard social norms guiding transitions that can start in their early twenties but often not resolve until their late thirties or forties.[3] While prior generations in their twenties could rely on standard norms in a specific order, this has been replaced by endless options with little structure.

For example, many members of our young adult research team have parents who followed the order of attending college, getting jobs, getting married, buying houses, and having children. Nearly all of this occurred by the time they were thirty. By contrast, we are part of a generation that has options such as taking gap years, pursuing graduate degrees, moving to different states and countries, and taking birth control. Not only are these options more readily available to us than previous generations, but many in this age group today are also facing several challenges from the job market, housing costs, and tuition rates that make the order previously described nearly impossible to achieve. Due to its pursuit of higher education, residential instability and wide scope of social (e.g., choice of friend groups) and intellectual (e.g., choice of college majors) experiences, our twentysomething age group is demographically different from surrounding ages.[4]

Young adults are exposed to multiple options for community, such as school, family, faith community. They can be selective about which

3. Jeffrey J. Arnett, "Emerging Adulthood: A Theory of Development from the Late Teens through the Twenties," *American Psychologist* 55, no. 5 (2000): 469–80, https://doi.org/10.1037//0003-066x.55.5.469.

4. Jeffrey J. Arnett, "College Students as Emerging Adults: The Developmental Implications of the College Context," *Emerging Adulthood* 4, no. 3 (2015): 219–22.

of their core values (e.g., relationships and belonging, unique contribution, autonomy) are met by which communities.[5] Along with this increase in choice, young adults today are significantly less likely to attend religious services than other age groups and in lower numbers than prior generations.[6] They are in a stage that heavily determines much identity and direction, and they are often distanced from a Christian religious community.

In this turbulent time of life, tasked with determining their adult identities and beliefs, today's young adults have specific needs and values that are determined by both their life stage and current context. Even among Christian young adults, there are diverse approaches to spirituality and religion. This presents churches with an opportunity to listen to the young adults in their communities and support them in their spiritual and developmental journeys.

Young Adults and Religious Affiliation

Young adults have a lower rate of religious affiliation today than any other age group, and the rate is lower than that of earlier generations at their age.[7] In 2015, approximately 33 percent of Americans under thirty years of age identified as religiously unaffiliated, whereas for Generation X, the baby boomers, and the silent generation it was 23 percent, 17 percent, and 11 percent, respectively.[8] Furthermore, while research indicates that young adults' spiritual beliefs and practices are similar to previous generations, they are less likely to be

5. Angie Thurston and Casper ter Kuile, "How We Gather: The Rise of Unaffiliated Millennials," Harvard Divinity School and Crestwood Foundation report, 2015, https://caspertk.files.wordpress.com/2015/04/how-we-gather1.pdf.

6. Phil Zuckerman, Luke W. Galen, and Frank L. Pasquale, *The Nonreligious: Understanding Secular People and Societies* (New York: Oxford University Press, 2016).

7. Zuckerman, Galen, and Pasquale, *The Nonreligious*.

8. Pew Research Center, "America's Changing Religious Landscape," online report, https://www.pewresearch.org/religion/2015/05/12/americas-changing-religious-landscape/.

part of an organized religion.[9] We even saw this in how many of the churches participating in Pivot Northwest mentioned that membership in their congregations was no longer formal and was replaced with a more general sense of relationship or belonging.

Young Adults' Approach to Spirituality: Research Overview

To understand religious and spiritual beliefs among young adults, an important place to begin is with the *National Study of Youth and Religion* (NSYR). Two of the researchers involved in the NSYR identified five consistent categories of adolescent religiosity: abiders, adapters, assenters, avoiders, and atheists.[10] Abiders, the most traditionally "religious" group, were identified as having "consistent involvement in religious practices, belief in a personal God, and a high level of religious importance in their own lives."[11] On the other end of the spectrum, atheists were identified by expressing disbelief in God. The researchers noted that those in the atheist group were actively and consistently nonreligious, distinguishing them from others who displayed passive disinterest in religion. Despite holding completely different beliefs, the atheists and the abiders were similar in that they had the most consistent responses; atheists were entirely nonreligious across all areas studied, while abiders were entirely religious.

The three remaining categories—adapters, assenters, and avoiders—were characterized by their lack of consistency. Assenters, for

---

9. Luis Lugo, "Religion among the Millennials: Less Religiously Active than Older Americans, but Fairly Traditional in Other Ways," A Pew Forum on Religion & Public Life report, 2010, http://assets.pewresearch.org/wp-content/uploads/sites/11/2010/02/millennials-report.pdf; Richard D. Waters and Denise Sevick Bortree, "Can We Talk about the Direction of This Church? The Impact of Responsiveness and Conflict on Millennials' Relationship with Religious Institutions," *Journal of Media and Religion* 11, no. 4 (2012): 200–215.

10. Lisa D. Pearce and Melinda Denton, *A Faith of Their Own: Stability and Change in the Religiosity of America's Adolescents* (New York: Oxford University Press, 2011).

11. Pearce and Denton, *A Faith of Their Own*, 34.

example, expressed belief in God and reported participation in religious activities, but they did not indicate that religion or spirituality were central to their lives. Adapters expressed belief in God but showed varying levels of outward religious participation; however, they reported that their faith was very important to them, and they showed a strong tendency to think about the meaning of life and help others around them. Finally, avoiders expressed a belief in God but showed very little interest or participation in religion. While these three categories each have a unique profile of religiosity, they all show that religious belief and participation are not clear-cut; young people can engage (or not engage) with religion in a variety of ways.

To better understand young adult religiosity, our team from Pivot NW Research designed a study aiming to replicate these categories in young adults using a sample of Christian young adults. In our study, we found that while all the young adults we surveyed identified as Christian, their approaches to religion mirrored the approaches found in the NSYR (abiders, adapters, assenters, and avoiders), reflecting significant differences in personal religious beliefs, faith practices, and faith maturity.[12] See Table 1 on page 43 for category descriptions.

What Takeaways Can We Glean from This Research?

This research should inform our understanding of how young adults approach religion. Not all Christian young adults are abiders. Some are adapters, prioritizing a more flexible kind of religiosity. Some are assenters, who believe in God but may be more distant from religion and spirituality. Some might be avoiders, unsure about God and having little religious participation but valuing religion and spirituality nonetheless. While your first instinct might be (like mine) to label abiders as the ideal group and to view young adults in the other categories as either misguided or en route to becoming abiders, consider

---

12. Mathea Krogstad, Gabrielle Metzler, Paul Yost, and Mackenzie Allison, "Beyond the Pews: A Multidimensional Approach to Young Adults' Faith Development" (unpublished manuscript, 2022).

that these diverse approaches to religiosity may be adaptive, responding to a society moving away from organized religion, rather than problematic. This is seen nowhere more prominently in the United States than in the Pacific Northwest.

TABLE 1: Comparison of Latent Classes of Young Adults' Religiosity[13]

	Abiders	Adapters	Assenters	Avoiders
Belief in God	Believes in God	Believes in God	Believes in God	Is unsure of belief in God
View of God	Sees God as a personal being	Sees God as a personal being, or possibly as an impersonal being or force	Sees God as a personal being, or possibly as an impersonal being or force	Sees God as a cosmic life force, or possibly as an impersonal being
View of truth in religion	Believes truth is only in Christianity	Believes there may be truth in many religions	Believes there may be truth in many religions	May believe that truth is in many religions or no religion
View of religious beliefs	Believes that religious beliefs must be taken as a whole	Believes that it's OK to pick and choose religious beliefs	Believes that it's OK to pick and choose religious beliefs	Believes that it's OK to pick and choose religious beliefs
Praying alone	Prays alone frequently	Prays alone frequently	Prays alone occasionally	Prays alone occasionally
Church attendance	Attends church regularly	May attend church occasionally or regularly	Attends church occasionally	Attends church occasionally

13. Table from Krogstad et al., "Beyond the Pews."

	Abiders	Adapters	Assenters	Avoiders
Helping others	Helps others frequently	Likely to help others frequently	Helps others frequently	Helps others frequently
Importance of religion	Sees religion as being highly important	Probably sees religion as being highly important	Sees religion as being mildly important	Sees religion as being highly important
Closeness to God	Feels very close to God	Probably feels very close to God	Feels somewhat close to or distant from God	Probably feels distant from God
Thinking about the meaning of life	Thinks about the meaning of life occasionally or often	Probably thinks about the meaning of life often	Thinks about the meaning of life occasionally	Thinks about the meaning of life occasionally or often

How Do We Understand the Variation in Christian Faith Practices among Self-identified Christian Young Adults?

The Pacific Northwest, dubbed the "None Zone" for being the region with the most people identifying their religious affiliation as "none," is an excellent example of a place where society has shifted from religion toward postmodern, socially constructed worldviews.[14] As young adult graduate students attending a Christian university in this None Zone, we (the authors) have experienced this secular culture firsthand. Even having grown up as a pastor's daughter (Mathea) and the daughter of missionaries (Gabrielle), we, along with many others in our research team, have spent the early years of our young adulthood navigating the tension between religious and secular, traditional and postmodern. In

14. Patricia O'Connell Killen and Mark Silk, *Religion and Public Life in the Pacific Northwest: The None Zone* (Lanham: AltaMira, 2004).

the Pacific Northwest, as in many urban centers, the cultural shift from organized religion toward personal spirituality is apparent.

Dietrich Bonhoeffer, a pastor and theologian in the mid-twentieth century, identified this cultural shift over half a century ago and asked what it meant for Christians:

> What is bothering me incessantly is the question [of] what Christianity really is, or indeed who Christ really is, for us today. The time when people could be told everything by means of words, whether theological or pious, is over and so is the time of inwardness and conscience—and that means the time of religion in general. We are moving towards a completely religionless time; people as they are now simply cannot be religious any more. . . . How can Christ become the Lord of the religionless as well? Are there religionless Christians? If religion is only a garment of Christianity—and even this garment has looked very different at different times—then what is a religionless Christianity? . . . What do a church, a community, a sermon, a liturgy, a Christian life mean in a religionless world? How do we speak of God—without religion, i.e., without the temporally conditioned presuppositions of metaphysics, inwardness, and so on? How do we speak (or perhaps we cannot now even 'speak' as we used to) in a 'secular' way about 'God'? In what way are we 'religionless-secular' Christians, in what way are we . . . called forth, not regarding ourselves from a religious point of view as specially favoured, but rather as belonging wholly to the world? In that case Christ is no longer an object of religion, but something quite different, really the Lord of the world. But what does that mean? What is the place of worship and prayer in a religionless situation?[15]

Although this letter was written from a prison in Nazi Germany in 1944, Bonhoeffer could have just as easily written these words about

---

15. Dietrich Bonhoeffer, *Letters and Papers from Prison* (London: SCM, 2017), 279–81.

the Pacific Northwest today. He identified questions that have become only more relevant since he asked them: What does it mean to be Christian in a nonreligious world? And what meaning do the behaviors and practices of Christianity have in a world without religion? To Christian young adults in a secular society, these questions from eighty years ago feel surprisingly pertinent.

As we saw in the findings of multiple research studies, many young adults—including Christians—are spiritually engaged even if not traditionally religious. Bonhoeffer might say that this is evidence of a secular society's changing interpretation of an unchanging God—that while the way we approach religion changes, God's truth is still at the center. From this perspective, churches can find great value through engaging with young adults where they are.

Faith Communities and Young Adult Values

While it is clear that young adults today are not connecting with faith communities as much as previous generations did, the research on why is limited.[16] One potential reason for the disconnect could be the lack of structure and social norms guiding this phase of life in general, as we discussed above.

In one interview with a church participating in the Pivot NW Research study, church leaders echoed this lack of structured societal norms for young adults, and one of them said "One of the questions we've been asking ourselves is, how do you bring these young adults under one umbrella? Cause some of them [are] just getting out of high school and then some of them are just joining college. Some of them are in college, almost finishing up, and then others are working and single. Others are dating or going to grad school now. And then we

16. Jean M. Twenge and Stacy M. Campbell, "Generational Differences in Psychological Traits and Their Impact on the Workplace," *Journal of Managerial Psychology* 23 (2008): 862–77; Zuckerman, *The Nonreligious*.

have young married couples." On top of this lack of role constraints, young adults have more options for community than before.

When interviewed, many in our participating churches highlighted the challenge of young adults being very busy. They mentioned that young adults often go from event to event and have plenty of options for finding community—especially since the internet makes this a very connected world. When the church is viewed through the young adult lens of time and commitment, it becomes challenging to justify prioritizing church over other community options that they find more fulfilling.

While the church may not currently be the top choice for young adults to find fulfillment, churches can leverage the core values they provide to better meet young adults' needs and become communities that engage and enable them. When asked how they defined faithfulness, one of our Pivot NW Research church leaders stated, "I hope that what is one of the benchmarks for our faithfulness is that there is a movement of [twentysomethings], that age group, finding their stride, their voice, their importance, their agency. Connecting that to faith. And that this community can be part of helping that to happen." We heard this same sentiment throughout our discussions with many churches, which is why this topic of communities and values was so important for us to dive into.

Young Adult Values and the Church: Survey Results

As part of our grant, we researched the question of "Which young adult values are uniquely fulfilled by faith communities?" To do this, we aimed to identify (1) what young adults value, (2) the places where those values are met, and (3) the role Christian faith communities can play in meeting those values. The following includes a description of how we conducted our survey, the results we found, and what this may mean for church communities looking to engage young adults.

Subjects

Our sample consisted of participants between the ages of twenty-three to twenty-nine ($M = 28$, $SD = 1.91$) and was focused on participants in the Pacific Northwest (44 percent) with the other 56 percent of participants residing in other regions of the United States. Our sample included participants between the ages of twenty-three to twenty-nine years of age ($M = 28$, $SD = 1.91$) with approximately 44.5 percent males and 54.8 percent females who identified as 72.8 percent Caucasian or white, 6.7 percent African American or Black, 5.3 percent Hispanic or Latino, 6.5 percent Asian, and 8.7 percent multiracial with 53 percent attending a Christian (Catholic, non-denominational, or Protestant) faith community, and 33 percent not attending any faith community. Sample distribution was in line with the demographic distribution in the Pacific Northwest based on most recent US Census Bureau data.

On-Ramps and Off-Ramps

In our survey we asked emerging adults to identify on-ramps and off-ramps that either invite or discourage participation in faith communities. With regard to on-ramps, the top five on-ramps were that (1) people in churches seem to care about each other, (2) church is a way to get involved in helping poor and disadvantaged people, (3) church is an opportunity to meet people, (4) church is an opportunity to deal with grief and loss, and (5) respondents feel welcomed by the leaders in the church (e.g. pastors). In regard to off-ramps, emerging adults in our study said the top five barriers to moving into deeper commitment and community were that (1) church faith communities are resistant to change, (2) respondents tend to have political views that are in disagreement with Christian faith communities, (3) people in Christian faith communities are hypocritical and judgmental, (4) the leaders in Christian faith communities are hypocritical, and (5) Christian faith communities do not create spaces to talk about real or controversial issues.

While emerging adults may self-report other reasons as the most significant predictors of their attendance and participation in church, the data from our surveys suggests that emerging adults in the United States who agree with several particular statements are more likely to attend church frequently (on a scale with 1= predicts attendance perfectly and 0 = does not predict attendance at all). Data gathered is from a combined sample of those surveyed in the United States and Pacific Northwest (N = 417), and all correlations are significant at the .01 level (2 tailed). The statements are: "Church is essential for my growth as a person" (r = 0.681); "Fellowship with other people is important" (r = 0.656); "Church feels like 'home'" (r = 0.594); "My family attends church" (r = 0.526); and "I feel welcomed by the leaders in the church" (r = 0.522). As a counterpoint, emerging adults in the United States who agree with the following statements are less likely to attend church frequently: "Churches are not authentic and transparent spaces" (r = 0.558); "Church does not help me develop spiritually" (r = 0.553); "Christianity doesn't adequately address suffering, cruelty, or injustice in the world" (r = 0.532); "Church is not a space where I feel I can build meaningful relationships" (r = 0.510); and "I feel like I do not have a voice in the church" (r = 0.505).

These statements demonstrate the importance of community, connection, and opportunity for growth for young adults seeking involvement in faith communities. This observation aligns with what we discovered when we asked young adults about their values.

What Does Church Provide for Emerging Adults?

We asked young adults what their top values are and where those values were being met. Top values were assessed based on ratings of importance and satisfaction. Data were gathered from a combined sample of emerging adults in the United States and Pacific Northwest (N = 296). These were the top values we discovered:

TABLE 2: *Values and Definitions*

Value	Definition(s) in Literature	Our Definition
Purpose and meaning	Purpose: "People's identification of, and intention to pursue, particular highly valued, overarching life goals."[17] Meaning: "The sense made of, and significance felt regarding, the nature of one's being and existence."[18]	I value having a sense of purpose, direction and meaning in life.
Spiritual growth	Spirituality: "Connection to self-chosen and or religious beliefs, values, and practices that give meaning to life, thereby inspiring and motivating individuals to achieve their optimal being."[19] Spirituality: "Believing in a higher power, cultivating loving relationships, being involved in good works in a social/civic context, trying to be eco-friendly."[20]	I value developing higher awareness and consciousness, engaging in spiritual practices (meditation, prayer, etc.), acknowledging a higher power or god.

17. M. F. Steger and B. J. Dik, "Work as Meaning: Individual and Organizational Benefits of Engaging in Meaningful Work," in *Oxford Handbook of Positive Psychology and Work*, ed. P. A. Linley, S. Harrington, and N. Page (Oxford: Oxford University Press, 2010), 133.

18. M. F. Steger, P. Frazier, S. Oishi, and M. Kaler, "The Meaning in Life Questionnaire: Assessing the Presence of and Search for Meaning in Life," *Journal of Counseling Psychology* 53 (2006): 81.

19. R. A. Tanyi, "Towards Clarification of the Meaning of Spirituality," *Journal of Advanced Nursing* 39 (2002): 506.

20. D. O. Berger, "On Means, Ends, and Millennials," *Missio Apostolica: Journal of the Lutheran Society for Missiology* 21, no. 41 (2013): 12.

Value	Definition(s) in Literature	Our Definition
Personal transfor-mation	Personal transformation: "Making a conscious and dedicated effort to develop one's own body, mind, and spirit."[21]	I value being able to develop and connect my body, mind, and spirit.
Peace	Self-acceptance: "Holding positive attitudes toward oneself."[22] Work-life balance: "Not sacrificing life for work . . . integrating the two."[23]	I value self-acceptance, restoration, and relaxation.
Fun	Creativity: "Allowing time and space to activate the imagination and engage in play."[24]	I value allowing time and space to be creative, adventurous, and to play.
Autonomy	Controlling: "To feel effective in dealing with their social environment and themselves."[25] Independence: "Making independent decisions." "Becoming financially independent." "Independent exploration of possible life directions."[26]	I value my independence and the capability to make my own decisions.

21. Thurston and ter Kuile, "How We Gather," 8.

22. C. D. Ryff, "Happiness Is Everything, or Is It? Explorations on the Meaning of Psychological Well-Being," *Journal of Personality and Social Psychology* 57 (1989): 1071.

23. Gallup Inc., "How Millennials Want to Work and Live," Gallup Inc. report, 2016, 31, https://www.gallup.com/workplace/238073/millennials -work-live.aspx.

24. Thurston and ter Kuile, "How We Gather," 8.

25. S. T. Fiske, *Social Beings: Core Motives in Social Psychology*, 2nd ed. (Hoboken, NJ: John Wiley & Sons, 2010), 20.

26. Jeffrey J. Arnett, "Emerging Adulthood: A Theory of Development from the Late Teens through the Twenties," *American Psychologist* 55, no. 5 (2000): 473, 478. https://doi.org/10.1037//0003-066x.55.5.469.

Value	Definition(s) in Literature	Our Definition
Stability	Financial well-being: "Having enough money to live the kind of life one wants to live and building financial security."[27] Job security: "Reliable jobs with stable companies."[28]	I value job security, financial security (for both my needs and wants), commitment to people or organizations with a solid reputation and pattern of growth.
Relationships and belonging	Positive relations with others: "Warm, trusting interpersonal relations."[29] Community: "Valuing and fostering deep relationships that center on service to others."[30] Belonging: "The idea that people need strong, stable relationships with other people."[31]	I value warm satisfying relationships, accountability, and belonging; I value being accepted by others even when discussing difficult topics.
Unique contribution	Controlling: "To feel effective in dealing with their social environment and themselves."[32] Recognizing contribution: "Does this organization value my strengths and my contribution?"[33]	I value having my personal significance recognized by others and adding value to a group or community, being seen by others, having mastery.

27. Gallup, "How Millennials Want to Work and Live," 86.
28. Gallup, "How Millennials Want to Work and Live," 31.
29. Ryff, "Happiness Is Everything, or Is It?," 1071.
30. Thurston and ter Kuile, "How We Gather," 8.
31. Fiske, *Social Beings*, 17.
32. Fiske, *Social Beings*, 20.
33. Gallup, "How Millennials Want to Work and Live," 4.

Value	Definition(s) in Literature	Our Definition
Social transformation	Social transformation: "Pursuing justice and beauty in the world through the creation of networks for good."[34]	I value helping others in need, pursuing justice and beauty in the world through the creation of networks for good, a chance to be part of something bigger than myself.
Networking	Networking: "Building networks of advisors and co-creators across sectors."[35] Social media use: "Use of social media to . . . connect with friends and family . . . find others who have similar interests or careers . . . network of search for a job."[36]	I value having access to networks of organizations, mentors, career development assistants, and people with similar interests; use of social networks to find community.

We found that emerging adults have less satisfaction with the church's overall ability to fulfill all eleven values, with the exception of spiritual growth. While this might seem problematic in relation to meeting felt needs and top values, it is important to note that emerging adults exist in a broad ecosystem of support and meaning-making. In surveying emerging adults, a number of "third places" arose as vital for emerging adult thriving. In listing their most common and important third places beyond work and family, they noted going to the gym; outdoor activities; value-based social groups; and exercise classes and sports such as yoga, Crossfit, Zumba, and soccer.

When asked specifically what the church provides that is distinctive from other places such as family, work, and assorted third places,

34. Thurston and ter Kuile, "How We Gather," 8.
35. Thurston and ter Kuile, "How We Gather," 12.
36. Gallup, "How Millennials Want to Work and Live," 77.

the following three values rose to the top: spiritual growth, peace, and social transformation. These values are somewhat uniquely fulfilled by the church as they did not show up as top values for many other places. While peace is a value that young adults are fulfilling via places other than Christian faith communities, spiritual growth and social transformation were not strongly fulfilled by other places, making them church differentiators.[37]

One way that churches can support young adults in this stage of life is by leveraging the fact that they are uniquely qualified to fulfill these values. For example, young adults value peace but are likely to find that value met more by their yoga group than by the church. What would it look like if the church were to invest in creating moments of peace during a sermon to better meet this young adult need? Or what would it look like if a church fully invested in social transformation and partnered with young adults in their community to do so?

We saw many examples of these sorts of value-driven innovations from our church partners. One young adult group created an outdoor prayer labyrinth in the church parking lot after the murder of George Floyd in 2020. Knowing that their church and larger community was grieving, they created a space for people to experience a moment of peace. Interestingly, this act seemed to provide an opportunity to meet all three needs—peace, spiritual growth, and social transformation—as people gathered for prayer and reflection in solidarity.

Another church partner held monthly virtual gatherings during the pandemic where people worked on creative projects together. Each gathering involved a guiding reflection as well as unstructured time during which people wrote poetry, sketched, played music, or spent time in contemplation. This peaceful space provided a sense of unity at a time when community connection was severely threatened.

37. Gabrielle Metzler, Mathea Krogstad, Paul Yost, Jeff Keuss, Mackenzie Allison, and Kait Hemphill, "Faith Community Differentiators: The Unique Role of Faith Communities for Young Adults" (unpublished manuscript, 2022).

The participants even transformed the art projects created during these times into a book titled *A Creative Anthology from Pandemic Times* that the community could share with others. These are just two examples of churches employing creative means to engage the values of young adults. We were continually impressed and inspired by the innovative practices of our church partners.

How Do Emerging Adults Grow in Their Faith at Church?

Since spiritual growth is a church differentiator, we decided to dig deeper into what spiritual growth might involve. We sought to answer the question of what practices individuals engage in that grow and deepen their faith. In our survey, we used a scale that located nine faith practices that seemed to build a sustaining faith over time, as self-reported by the participants in the Pacific Northwest sample combined with the US sample ($N = 352$). The nine practices that rose to the top were: reading scripture ($r = 0.463$), prayer ($r = 0.449$), worship (0.414), communion (0.369), confession ($r = 0.343$), journaling ($r = 0.321$), fasting (0.294), meditation (0.245), and caring for others (0.284). Churches seeking to deepen young adult faith should find ways to help young adults regularly engage these practices. Some successful examples we saw from our church partners were annual coat drives to help homeless neighbors, small groups that talked through Scripture together, weekly prayer gatherings, and participation in seasonal liturgical practices.

Additionally, when young adults are involved in a church, three types of practices are seen as contributing to ongoing faith growth: faith growth practices (33 percent), community-building practices (14 percent), and practices for openness (12 percent). While other assorted factors (41 percent) were noted, these three were dominant and overlapped across the survey:

- Faith growth practices: These are seen as those active engagements that personally embodied and reinforced belief in ways that created connections with others. Examples of faith growth practices include: helping people with religious questions, acting in ways that reflect a commitment to Jesus Christ, talking openly with people about faith, and taking responsibility for reducing the pain and suffering in the world.

- Community-building practices: These are seen as moving faith growth practices into communal accountability for the deepening of faith. Examples include: treating others in the community like family, acceptance and inclusion of newcomers, connecting with one another outside of programmed events in church, and helping people continue to feel like essential parts of the congregation.

- Practices for openness: These represent commitment to innovation and diversity in all aspects of communal and personal life. Examples include: showing that the community tries new approaches and listens for new ideas, demonstrating a willingness to change the way things are done, actively sharing and listening to different points of view, and making it safe to express doubts and concerns about the church.

Fortunately for churches, spiritual growth practices are embedded in their DNA. Churches do not have to completely change who they are to meet this particular young adult value. Scripture reading, prayer, communion, and other practices of faith growth are already regular parts of most churches' existence. Being intentional about these practices and being open to new ways of engaging spiritual growth will help churches connect with and support the needs of young adults.

Conclusion

There is no "one way" that young adults are approaching Christianity and their faith. As described earlier, emerging adulthood is a time when young adults are defining their identities, including their religious and spiritual identities. For young adults who desire to live out their faith in a church community, this is an essential time for them to find support and guidance from churches. In later chapters, we will discuss ways churches can accompany young adults during this tumultuous season of life—serving as resource stations, providing opportunities for leadership growth, and developing new forms of church engagement. We hope this work encourages churches to find ways to meet young adults where they are, taking their values and needs into consideration, and understanding that as the world changes, the ways young adults approach Christianity are changing, too.

Chapter Reflection Questions

1. How might you partner with young adults and support them in navigating this stage of life while still providing them the space to explore their spiritual and religious identities?

2. What values do young adults go to your church to meet and fulfill? How have you leaned into (or how could you lean into) supporting these values?

3. Looking at the immediate context of young adults in your community, what are some key challenges they are facing?

4. Looking at Table 1, do any of the four groups remind you of the young adults in your congregation? In your community? If so, how do you engage with these young adults where they are?

5. How has your church adapted to the societal shifts away from organized religion and toward socially constructed worldviews? How do you see your young adults navigating the cultural divide between traditional Christianity and modern thought?

3

Deep Listening and Young Adults

Thematic Analysis

LAUREN ST. MARTIN

At least ten young adults crammed into the living room of an apartment. Sitting on the couches, on the floors, they huddled around the microphone, ready to answer questions about their church and the young adult group that had been thriving there for years. They talked about the deep friendships they'd developed, their hopes for the young adult group, conflicts that arose with church leadership. They laughed, ate pizza, and drank La Croix.

A pastor and his wife sat down across from the microphone, smiling, as always, but frustrated. They so deeply desired to invest in the lives of young adults and, one after another, it seemed like each young person with whom they connected had a different reason to leave. The second their efforts to develop a young adult group got traction, something would happen to put them right back at the starting line.

At this table, two of the three pastors were young adults and all three were men of color. The eldest had started the church plant as an outreach effort to young adults and now they were moving into the church building of an aging congregation that could no longer manage it. The pastors told stories of how they were connecting well with their multiethnic neighborhood, but also how the new life they brought was so different for the older congregants that none of them stayed long.

———

One way that Pivot NW Research supported the churches with which we partnered was to provide consulting, helping churches reflect on the past and envision possibilities for the future. This consulting took the form of annual interviews over the course of four years with those involved in the young adult programs—pastors, older lay leaders, young adult leaders, or other participants. In total, we collected and analyzed over thirty-five hours of interviews with ten churches focused on three years of data collection.

During each interview, the program manager and director posed a series of questions meant to guide the group in the process of self-reflection. This was a form of qualitative research called "thematic analysis" where the focus was not on quantitative data collection but on having generative conversations with our churches to encourage them in their innovation. This meant that while these questions often had similar themes, they varied, allowing for the flexibility to adjust to each church's particular situation and allowing for natural conversations.

At the end of each year, the ethnographic data was collected and distilled. To guide the process of our thematic analysis, we relied on the phases provided by Virginia Braun and Victoria Clarke: familiarizing ourselves with the data, generating initial codes, searching for themes, reviewing themes, defining and naming themes, and producing the report.[1] We added some additional protocols to these phases. First,

1. Virginia Braun and Victoria Clarke, "Using Thematic Analysis in Psy-

the interviews were transcribed, then we input the transcripts into spreadsheets such that each cell represented a single cohesive thought. After that, each member of the ethnography team read the transcripts and took notes regarding themes and important quotes. The individual spreadsheets were then sent to one team member to compile into a single spreadsheet. The team member compiling the spreadsheet read each person's notes and suggested themes, noting those potential themes in one column. That person focused on themes that were repeated throughout the interview and were represented in multiple team members' notes. The compiled spreadsheet was then sent out to all team members who each searched for themes and subthemes.

These themes were then refined. Team members met for a two-hour period in which they presented their individual thematic maps, looked for themes that could be dropped due to lack of data support and for themes that could be further broken down into subthemes. Then they read through transcripts a second time to ensure themes were appropriate for their respective contexts. When refinements failed to add anything substantial, the map was considered complete. This resulted in a final thematic map. Additionally, these themes were considered as they related to the entire data set and were recorded in a codebook that could be used when coding other interviews.

Themes were divided among team members. Using the transcripts and notes, each team member was responsible for renaming their themes (if necessary) and providing a one-sentence definition of the theme. Additionally, each member wrote short paragraphs summarizing each of their themes and subthemes, and described the relationships between the themes. Team members then included two relevant quotes from the transcript for each of their themes. This information was then transferred into a final report that was shared with the church.

chology," *Qualitative Research in Psychology* 3 (2006): 77–101, http://dx.doi .org/10.1191/1478088706qp063oa.

These individual church reports were later synthesized into a larger report that summarized the common themes found across different church contexts. This was done by year, and those yearly reports were all combined into a final thematic analysis for the whole project. Clear themes emerged across all the churches.

The following is an explanation of the biggest themes from all three years of interviews and information on how they might be important for other churches wishing to engage in this work.

Listening to and Obeying God

The first theme that emerged from our conversations with churches was *listening to and obeying God*. This was described as both the calling and the aim of a church. For our churches, listening included such practices as studying the Bible, meditating on Jesus, and spending time with the Holy Spirit. These listening practices led to a better understanding of God's will. Once churches understood God's will, they felt called to obey that will. One way they could obey God was through stewardship of their physical resources including buildings, land, and money. They also expressed a call to steward the gifts and talents of their people, particularly the young adults with whom they were connecting. Finally, obedience encompassed the Great Commission, reaching out to the unchurched or dechurched to help them connect with the love of Christ through the church.

The importance of grounding this work with young adults in the spiritual life of the church cannot be overstated. Engaging young adults should be an act of obedience to the church's calling, not a response to cultural pressures or fears. As with any ministry, prayerful consideration and reflection are important. Consider gathering a team of people who commit to pray regularly for the ministry of your church and specifically your current or potential engagement with young adults. Perhaps your discernment will lead to the discovery of a business around the corner that primarily employs young adults. Or perhaps your discernment will lead you to recognize that your church is not in a position to welcome young adults at this time.

Spiritual Formation

Spiritual formation was highlighted as one of the most important and unique roles of the church, as stated in the previous chapter. Interviewees described it as listening to the Holy Spirit and following the Spirit's leadership in equipping and empowering young adults to be good disciples and to disciple others. Two key aspects of spiritual formation are discipleship and listening to the Spirit. Discipleship emphasizes interpersonal connection, whereas listening to the Spirit emphasizes connection with God. Spiritual formation is an act of faithfulness, as it deepens and strengthens faith in God. Perhaps unsurprisingly, spiritual formation was also connected to church growth. It was seen as an important pathway for equipping and empowering young adults to share Christ's love as teachers and ministers within the church and in the wider world.

While many viewed the Holy Spirit as the source of discernment and guidance, there was a strong emphasis on the importance of spiritual formation taking place in relationship, as mature Christians took responsibility for training those in earlier stages of faith growth and those in earlier stages spent time learning from and with those who had more knowledge of the Bible and spiritual practices. Being a mature Christian is not tied to age but rather to desire and training. As a result, many churches hoped to equip young adults to lead and disciple one another and older adults.

Being intentional about spiritual formation, through small groups or discipleship programs, is one of the most important things you can do for young adults and for the life of your church. Many young adults want to grow spiritually, and the church is in a unique position to help them do so. The church also needs to provide young adults access to positions of leadership so they can help guide the spiritual development of the church. Small groups and discipleship programs are good opportunities for young adults to take on leadership roles and to start integrating into the life of the church. As shown by the data in chapter 2, when churches embrace spiritual formation, faith growth and church sustainability begin to emerge.

Young Adult Needs

In each year of interviews, the importance of understanding and meeting young adult needs arose. Understanding young adult needs and values was both a means and an end for churches. As a means, it helps the church connect with young adults outside the church and better engage with young adults in the church. Since God desires people to be known, understood, and valued, this action was also a valued end in and of itself as well. In the first round of interviews, interviewees focused on identifying some important young adult needs. In the second and third rounds, there was more reflection on meeting those needs, as well as reflection from young adults on whether or not their needs were valued by the larger church.

The four main needs identified in the first interviews were (a) authenticity, (b) understanding young adult lifestyles, (c) understanding how young adults had been or could be wounded by the church, and (d) recognition of the fact that young adults do not want a fragile God.

Authenticity is highly valued by young adults. Young adults want to be loved and accepted without having to put up a facade or pretend to be someone they are not. When everyone practices authenticity, being honest about who they are, it reduces the complexity of modern life. It also helps young adults discover who they can trust in certain situations.

Young adult lifestyles reflect both internal values as well as the broader realities of the world young adults inhabit. The political, economic, technological, and environmental forces shaping young adults' daily experiences create pressure for them to be increasingly adaptable, mobile, and open-minded in order to access decent work, health care, affordable housing, and more. Young adult lifestyles are not homogeneous and vary widely by life stage, location, and personality, making it necessary for each church to intentionally get to know the young adults near them. When churches do not understand the broader context of young adult lives, they may conclude that young adult lifestyles fail to prioritize church above all else.

Young adults reported being *wounded by the church* as a major barrier to connecting and being fully involved with the church. For young adults who had been wounded, it was important to be able to acknowledge it and not be expected to hide or ignore the pain. Wounding can occur without intent or even with the best of intentions when someone fails to understand the needs and values of young adults.

Young adults do not want a fragile God. Young adults expressed wanting and needing a God with whom they could be honest and not have to feign certainty or agreement with church dogma. It was important to be able to wrestle with God not just privately but also publicly, as Jesus did on the cross when he asked, "My God, my God, why have you forsaken me?" (Matt. 27:46; Mark 15:34). This emerged as an especially important need and value when confronting issues like injustice and evil in the world.

The importance of social justice became even clearer in later interviews as social unrest expanded in 2020. Churches found that giving space for conversations about issues of race and justice led to deeper relationships, and churches that wrestled with and talked about issues of justice tended to see an increase in young adult engagement. Issues of justice, such as LGBTQIA+ inclusion or antiracism, were important to some churches' identities, which was an on-ramp for many young adults.

A couple other young adult needs identified in later interviews were *diversity* and *mentorship.*

As churches pursued social justice, young adults called on them to promote more *diversity* both in leadership and across the entire church body. Representation of different cultural and racial backgrounds is important for young adults and allows them to feel safe and included. Young adults desire diversity in the church in order to identify with others of similar experience due to racial or cultural commonalities. Diversity fosters a space for relationship building. Some multiethnic churches saw their diversity as an on-ramp, since many young adults want to be in diverse spaces and want to be part of churches that directly tackle issues of race, gender, and other justice issues.

Mentorship was another young adult need. Mentorship is vital for young adults in their faith, but it comes with challenges. Lack of commitment on the part of either the mentor or the young adult was one challenge. Some young adults also found they did not have genuine connections with their mentors. If the mentor relationship was not a good fit, finding a new mentor (almost like speed dating) was suggested in order to have a better connection and deeper relationship.

Meeting some young adult needs was admittedly difficult for churches. Mixing church traditions with the needs of young adults was challenging at every level of interaction. Often it was easier for people to leave or to stay in separate lanes than to create new common ground, especially when integration required crossing historical, racial, ethnic, or gender divides. While churches stated that they desired diversity, there was a strongly perceived lack of know-how when it came to navigating diversity, especially around issues of identity such as race, ethnicity, gender, and sexuality.

Churches interested in this work must try to better understand young adults and their needs. Understanding both the stage of life and the individual needs of young adults helps establish better relationships and ministries that are genuinely life-giving. But it is not enough to know young adult needs; churches need to be willing to change to meet those needs. Churches that are not willing to change will fail to be of interest to young adults.

The best way to learn about the needs of your young adults is to simply be in relationship with them. Sharing needs can be a vulnerable act, so it may take time before young adults are comfortable sharing themselves and their specific needs with you and your church community. However, it is good to be aware of the needs listed above since they seem to be generally applicable to those in the young adult stage of life.

Building Community

The theme of building community involves going beyond the church building and engaging the wider community in response to God's call to love and serve neighbors. While churches connected building community to the great commission, the primary emphasis was not on direct evangelism. Instead, churches focused on getting to know the people in the church's neighborhood and meeting their needs with cultural humility and intercultural competence. Another emphasis was engaging the larger political and social movements in pursuit of social justice, human rights, and equity. Only when the church has demonstrated its love through these acts of service can it effectively connect people with Christ. As the church builds up the people around it, it becomes a beacon of hope and a desired home.

Building community includes (a) outreach and connection with the broader community, (b) social justice, (c) the desire for diversity even when know-how is lacking, (d) making an impact on community culture, and (e) pivotal relationship-building moments.

Outreach and connection with the broader community could include physically relocating the church closer to the people it desires to serve, hosting community groups, or conducting outreach ministries for universities or homeless populations. Young adults were especially interested in participating in social justice events and learning more about how to do advocacy work.

As noted in young adult needs, *social justice* emerged as a pivotal issue since young adults want churches to fight for justice and equity, not just in the church but in the wider political, educational, and economic arenas. Whereas the church in America has often seen itself as more concerned with the state of a person's soul, young adults voiced concerns about people's physical and economic needs. Many believe that, as followers of Christ, those in the church cannot remain neutral or silent in the face of injustice. Many young adults see the reticence of the church to engage these issues as a major contributor to the exodus from the church by all ages. This theme is further nuanced in a later chapter.

Desiring diversity but lacking know-how is more than a barrier to integrating young adults within the church; it is also a barrier to reaching young adults outside the church. Reaching young adults outside the church requires more than a concern for their soul; it requires an appreciation and love for them as diverse people with cultures, languages, customs, and histories. Developing cultural humility and intercultural competencies is not easy and requires an investment of time and effort. Perhaps a litmus test for desiring diversity is whether a church invests in helping its people develop the knowledge and skills required to engage respectfully with the diversity in their particular community.

Making an impact on community culture means that a church's involvement in its community makes a difference. The more the church reflects the diversity of its neighborhood, the more likely it is to be able to interact in culturally life-giving ways. Members of the community are drawn to the church through its acts of love and the kind and generous conduct of its people.

Pivotal relationship-building moments for young adults were found in serving the community or fighting for social justice. Participating together in these activities forged bonds built on shared values and positive action. For churches looking to help young adults feel a sense of belonging and purpose, one of the best ways may be to create opportunities for them to serve their wider communities together.

Young adults want to be part of churches that care about their neighborhoods and the needs of those in their communities. Whether you have an established young adult group or you are looking to develop one, finding ways to reach out to your neighborhood is a key part of strengthening connections with and between young adults. Spend time locating an area of need in your community and find a way to meet that need—whether by partnering with an existing organization or creating your own service event or program. If you can, get the input of young adults in your congregation or community. Including young adults in the process will make your efforts more likely to gain traction.

Sustainability

Sustainability involves structures and practices that were already in place or were desired to maintain and grow young adult ministries. While the topic of young adult ministry growth arose in the first round of interviews, the theme of sustainability was much more prominent in later interviews as churches made further efforts to create, expand, or evolve their young adult communities.

The theme of sustainability arose in different ways. Many churches with young adult groups were considering what sorts of structures they should have in place to continue facilitating the growth and development of their groups as they welcomed new young adults and had some transition out. Even churches still in the process of establishing young adult groups were considering questions of sustainability. Each hoped to create something that had a better chance of lasting than their previous efforts.

Sustainability for our churches involved some or all of these facets: *structured programs, leadership, relational focus, creation of space,* and *good communication.*

In some cases, *good communication* meant leveraging technology to keep people connected. Social media platforms and group chat apps were mentioned in several interviews as ways to facilitate consistent communication.

Structured programs for young adults—places that provide support and easy connection—were important to churches. These structures often involved some of the following: regular gatherings, small groups, opportunities to serve local communities, conversations on issues of justice, and partnerships with local service organizations. Churches that had structured programs in place were going through iterations of innovation and learning how to let programs die when they were no longer helpful, even if they had been important in the past. The consensus was that churches needed to create flexible structures, leaving room for change.

While churches valued having structured programs in place where young adults could fit in, they also recognized the importance of a *relational focus*. Several churches tried creating programming for young adults but found there was very little interest. They had more success when they focused on reaching out to young adults as individuals, developing relationships with them first before trying to create systems into which they could fit. Programs could also be off-putting if they came on too strong or expected too much too soon. At the same time, simply waiting for organic relationships to occur did little to reassure newcomers that they were welcome and belonged.

A *relational focus* was consistently important for churches as both an on-ramp and a guardrail to keep young adults in church. Putting time and effort into developing relationships was a priority for churches that already had young adult connections and those seeking young adults. Responding to young adult needs was important for many churches and knowing their needs required having deep relationships with young adults. Focusing on relationships over programming was seen as an on-ramp for some churches, and a church's value was often tied to its ability to facilitate development of and growth in relationships.

Having *leadership*, from both young and older adults, that specifically took charge of the young adult program was also mentioned as a key part of sustainability. It was important for churches to have specific people to whom young adults could go with questions and needs. Some churches were at the point of hoping their current leaders would develop new leaders to share responsibilities or take them on as some aged out or moved to other ministries. Several churches demonstrated that sharing power led to better sustained ministries.

Spiritual growth and enrichment through young adult leadership and inclusion in the life of a church was seen as the key to sustainability as young adults were being mentored and nurtured, and as they gained experience in leading the church into the future. Having young adults feel free to grow in the church was seen as a sign of health and hope.

Creation of space that was hospitable and safe was an important part of developing relationships with young adults. Young adults value having a space in which they can comfortably be themselves—bringing their stories and their questions to the group. Many churches mentioned the importance of sharing testimonies and personal stories as a way to deepen relationships. Having conversations where people could get to know one another and discuss important topics led to vulnerability as people became comfortable sharing with one another. Issues of justice were mentioned, in particular, as topics that young adults wanted to talk about and which led to deeper connections. Small groups were important to many churches as safe spaces for relational development. Many young adults valued their small groups. These groups could serve as gateways to church connection, though this was not always the case.

While preparation for the future is important, there is no perfect structure that will guarantee sustainability—a reality that is difficult but crucial to accept. Focusing on relationships and being willing to adjust to the needs of your developing group is key. The structures that will be most sustainable are the ones that involve giving ownership and leadership to young adults.

Young Adult Leadership

Young adult leadership is crucial to the success of young adult ministries, setting the tone for engagement and culture in young adult communities. Young adult leadership seemed to be less formal than that of traditional church settings since young adults care less about formality. Instead, they want their leadership to seem inviting; anyone can be a leader if they are committed to it. Sponsorship from formal church leadership appeared to be important for the young adult leaders, though. Being mentored and cared for by the church helped young adult leaders feel safe to pursue new ideas.

Along with less formality, the structure of young adult leadership seemed less rigid than that of the larger church. If a young adult wanted to lead in some capacity, they were welcome to do so. A shared power structure where young adult leaders felt that they had ownership over their communities while also being supported by church leadership was important. When young adult leaders were allowed to take initiative and have ownership, their communities were more fruitful. However, commitment from new young adult leaders was sometimes a challenge for existing young adult leadership due to the transient nature of young adulthood.

Young adult leadership was seen as an especially challenging area for integration, as young adults' desire for autonomy and innovation sometimes clashed with existing leadership's need for more commitment to current practices. As a result, young adult leaders felt pressure to conform if they wanted to serve in senior roles and avoid being limited only to service in young adult ministries. Churches that were able to authentically integrate young adults into senior leadership and governance roles, however, benefited, as did the young adults. Having young adults take on leadership roles and engage in the mission of a church was seen as a sign of present health and hope for the future.

The church needs young adult leaders. Their unique perspectives and contributions will help the church navigate a world that is changing more rapidly now than at any other time in history. Churches that had the most success retaining young adult leaders were ones that provided a balance of autonomy and support. Young adults are ready to don the mantle of church leadership now, but they also desire and need mentorship. A helpful shift in perspective is thinking less in terms of leadership development and more in terms of leadership identification. Young adults are already leaders in many areas of their lives and already have leadership capacity. The church does not need to develop young leaders as much as it needs to identify and share power with these young adults. Chapter 5 will provide a more detailed explanation of the importance of leadership identification and mentorship for young adults.

Transition

Transition describes the temporariness of young adults within congregations or ministries due primarily to their geographical mobility and the life-stage pressures that keep them on the move during their twenties. The frequent transitions in young adults' lives are major challenges to building relationships and integrating young adults. While young adults often move for positive reasons such as graduate school, marriage, job offers, and promotion opportunities, moves can also be due to economic hardship or other difficult life circumstances.

Regardless of the reasons behind their moves, young adults often need churches that can support them in transition. To what degree are churches willing and able to be transition stations, and how do they integrate young adults who can connect only lightly or for a season?

Transition was presented mostly as a barrier to young adult involvement in church, but some positives were seen. Churches noted it was difficult to create sustainable young adult ministries when there was frequent churn. It was also hard to include transient young adults in leadership roles that required specific time commitments or levels of membership.

Transition also posed a barrier to forming and sustaining relationships among young adults. They described how difficult it was to sustain the energy needed to continuously build new relationships. Finding the energy was especially hard after a relationship failure, such as a mentor match that did not work out. Young adults described being put off by questions such as, "How long have you been going here?" which seemed to imply that their affiliation with the church was more important than who they were as people. Young adults sometimes felt that churches were waiting to see how often they showed up before investing in them.

It was an easy temptation for churches to expect young adults to leave and wait to see whether they would come back before investing in them. Young adults also found themselves sometimes embracing this waiting mindset, conserving relational energy for a time when they might be more settled as well. When attempted relationships failed, this strengthened the stereotype of young adults lacking commitment or being flaky. Older adults who were willing to mentor and invest in relationships sometimes experienced hurt and bewilderment if the relationships did not last. Some asked whether it was realistic to expect lasting relationships with young adults. Others questioned why young adults were leaving and wanted to know whether it was simply life circumstances or something in the church that had caused them to leave. When young adults simply stopped showing up without explaining their reasons for leaving, the behavior was sometimes described as "ghosting."

Despite many concerns about transition, it also had positive effects. Receiving congregations benefited from new ideas and the sharing of practices from other churches. Sending congregations were perceived as able to provide blessing and support to help ease the transition for those moving away. While it was acknowledged that transitions can be hard, young adults also appreciated the freedom to move on to churches that were better fits if things weren't working.

The way a church perceived transition made a difference in how young adults were engaged. Although cultural and economic forces were seen as key drivers of young adult transition, it was also noted that young adulthood itself is a transient phase, with people continually aging into it, through it, and out of it. This form of transition raised questions for churches about how to support young adults through these transitions that affect the core of young adult identity. Churches that can embrace young adult transition in multiple forms as a normal part of life may be able to help their members—and especially their young adults—navigate the challenges, comfort the sorrows, and experience the joys of transition more fully.

One church emphasized that young adult transition should not be seen as a barrier to spiritual formation. Instead, transition can be embraced as part of the process of making disciples who will go out and make more disciples. Equipping, empowering, and sending become ways of being open to the movement of the Holy Spirit and contributing to the sustainability of the church beyond the local congregation.

Transition is one of the most difficult challenges to navigate in young adult ministry. It is an important thing to acknowledge and plan for—so important that all of chapter 4 is devoted to this topic. Thinking about how your church approaches the transient nature of young adult life and having a plan—perhaps a sending ritual for young adults moving on to other opportunities or life stages—will help both the church and the young adults deal with transition.

Intergenerational Connection

Intergenerational connection involves the desire many churches developed to connect their young adults to the larger church body, creating more opportunities for them to serve and build relationships. As many churches developed their young adult groups, the desire arose to better connect these groups with their larger church communities. Some churches that started out with siloed young adult groups eventually wanted them to integrate into the church. In general, this did not mean doing away with young-adult-only spaces, which were still viewed as valuable. However, churches wanted young adults to have opportunities to get involved beyond those spaces—taking on leadership roles, volunteering in various ministries, and developing intergenerational relationships.

A large part of the desire for integration was recognizing the importance of intergenerational relationships. Seeking intergenerational community was even described as an act of faithfulness. Churches that had intergenerational community saw it as an opportunity for power sharing, an on-ramp for newcomers, and an opportunity for mentorship.

Mentorship was seen as important though challenging. Young adults voiced their desire to be part of a church family where surrogate grandparents, parents, and "aunties and uncles" provide support and encouragement, especially when young adults are far away from home. While these intergenerational relationships can lead to good, they can also cause harm if done poorly. Sometimes mentors are hurt by young adults' lack of commitment to these relationships. Young adults were sometimes hurt by being paired with older mentors who were not good fits for them. One interviewee noted that mentors from older generations will sometimes say things that offend their mentees. The topic of mentorship is further developed in chapter 5.

Several churches said they were struggling to develop the intergenerational community they wanted. Generational differences make it difficult to have healthy relational dynamics. For churches trying to attract young adults, having largely older populations in attendance was viewed as an off-ramp for young adults. However, the presence of older adults who wanted to welcome and invest in young adults was viewed as an on-ramp. While these complexities were acknowledged, most churches still viewed intergenerational community as important enough to pursue.

Intergenerational relationships are essential, not just for young adults but for everyone. While young-adult-only spaces are valuable, they cannot meet all the needs of young adults. The church has a unique opportunity to create intergenerational connections. Most of the other places young adults find community do not easily incorporate people from younger and older generations. Though there is no simple way to develop intergenerational community, acknowledging its importance is the first step.

Conclusion

All these themes—listening to and obeying God, spiritual formation, young adult needs, building community, sustainability, young adult leadership, transition, and intergenerational connection—are topics to keep in mind at all stages of your young adult ministry development. Whether you are laying the groundwork or discerning next steps for the third or fourth iteration of your ministry, these topics will always be pertinent.

You can use this list of themes to create reflection questions for your ministry team, questions you can come back to throughout the innovation process. We recognize that each church has its own set of circumstances, strengths, and challenges. The exact innovations of other churches may not work for you, but referencing these themes will encourage you to consider your blind spots and help you to craft your own strategies as you seek to faithfully respond to God's movement in the life of your church.

Chapter Reflection Questions

1. What does faithfulness mean to you and your church?
2. How does your church approach spiritual formation? What spiritual practices are important for your community?
3. What are the general demographics for your area? What might this tell you about young adult needs?
4. What are the needs of your local community? How might you meet them?
5. How do you go about developing relationships with young adults? What is your vision for young adult involvement at your church?
6. Do you have any young adults in positions of leadership at your church? If not, why? What might need to change to bring young adults into leadership?
7. Have you experienced the challenges of young adult transience? How have you handled it in the past? What might you do in the future?
8. What are some on-ramps and barriers to young adult involvement in your church?
9. What are some important characteristics for a good mentor? Who in your congregation would be a good mentor for young adults?

4

Church as Resource Station

Young Adults in Transition

LINDA MONTAÑO

The Olynnials are a group of young adults at a church in
Olympia, the capital city of Washington—hence the "Oly"
prefix. In February of 2020, they were thriving. They were
so excited about the many ways they were engaging each
other and their community. But within a year, the group
had lost all momentum. Their dynamic leader stepped back
to be more present with her young family; another leader
who was coming out of a raw personal battle felt a calling
to attend seminary in Atlanta; and, auspiciously, another
newlywed couple also transitioned to Atlanta when the
wife accepted her dream job at the Centers for Disease
Control and Prevention.

While a critical mass still existed beyond this handful of high-performing young adults who were throwing
themselves into the work of community building and faith
de- and reconstruction, the reality of young adult transience, perhaps compounded by the pandemic, had turned

their group into a shell of its former self. This demonstrates the sticky problem of transience that is so doggedly attached to being in the third decade of life, a time when young adults often find themselves rebuilding all of their social connections and constructing a foundation for the future.

—

The church has historically considered itself a place of support for people navigating transitions, yet young adults are turning elsewhere as they handle the many complex changes in their lives.[1] Rather than asking why this is the case, this chapter asks how churches might respond to this reality.

This chapter on living well amid the transitions of life is motivated by the theme of transition that stood out so strongly in Pivot NW Research's ethnographic work with churches in the Pacific Northwest. It was clear from this research that young adults are navigating a variety of simultaneous high-stakes transitions under conditions of increasing mobility due to technology and globalization,[2] and that this combination of forces is creating tremendous stress for young adults and churches alike.[3] The motivating questions that emerged over and over were, *What does it mean to live well in these transitions of life? To what degree is it even possible?*

These are important questions for everyone, but especially for young adults. A large-scale nationally representative study in the United

1. Tim Clydesdale and Kathleen Garces-Foley, *The Twentysomething Soul* (Oxford: Oxford University Press, 2019); Patricia O'Connell Killen and Mark Silk, *Religion and Public Life in the Pacific Northwest: The None Zone* (Lanham: AltaMira Press, 2004).

2. Lene A. Jensen and Jeffrey J. Arnett, "Going Global: New Pathways for Adolescents and Emerging Adults in a Changing World," *Journal of Social Issues* 68, no. 3 (2012): 473–92.

3. Clydesdale and Garces-Foley, *The Twentysomething Soul*.

States conducted from 2008 to 2017 reported that, among all adults, those ages eighteen to twenty-five had the greatest level of psychological distress.[4] This kind of distress included mood disorders, suicidal thoughts, self-harm, and suicide, and this group also experienced the highest growth rate in psychological distress over the course of the study at 78 percent. With the aim of helping to stem the tide of distress and to perhaps prevent it, this chapter examines why transitions in young adulthood can be so challenging and provides insight into multiple ways of living well that can be leveraged to make a difference. Our hope is that the ideas presented in this chapter will be a resource and an encouragement to anyone seeking to help young adults—and people of any age—experience the abundant and full life that God intends (John 10:10).

Before shining a spotlight on living well and examining transitions, it is necessary to revisit the definition of a young adult. While previous chapters provided commentary and deep insight on this, this chapter highlights some of the challenges that churches and young adults alike face in determining who exactly is in and who is out of this category. To illustrate the challenges, the next section of this chapter opens with some questions that may be familiar to anyone who has worked in young adult ministry.

Boundaries of Young Adulthood

Who is a young adult? Is it someone of a certain age? Is it determined by social status? Do they belong to a cohort? Are these interrelated, and if so, how and to what degree? Earlier chapters defined young adulthood as a particular life stage and explained common markers

---

4. J. M. Twenge, A. B. Cooper, T. E. Joiner, M. E. Duffy, and S. G. Binau, "Age, Period, and Cohort Trends in Mood Disorder Indicators and Suicide-Related Outcomes in a Nationally Representative Dataset, 2005–2017," *Journal of Abnormal Psychology* 128, no. 3 (2019): 185–99. https://doi.org/10.1037/abn0000410.

for what constitutes it. However, while explaining young adulthood is fairly clear, determining who fits into this category is less so. Young adults themselves grapple with this problem of identity and definition. This is perhaps most evident with young adult affinity groups. For example, young adult ministries have to decide how young is too young to qualify for a group and how old is too old to remain part of the group. Should there be separate groups for people who are married, divorced, or have children? What about young adults who are students versus working adults or those who are both?

Age is the easiest criterion to apply. A quick look at how several researchers have approached the question suggests an upper bound of twenty-nine and a somewhat fuzzier lower bound between eighteen and twenty-three.[5] Researchers who approach the question from a life-stage perspective sometimes divide the twenties at twenty-five. They suggest that before twenty-five, youth are approaching young adulthood, with the widest number of choices and decisions available to them, arriving fully at young adulthood at around twenty-five, with constraints from choices made during the earlier years influencing the rest of their twenties and beyond.[6] The life-stage perspective is nuanced and difficult to apply; even so, as we will see, there is fairly strong agreement among researchers about what constitutes the major life-stage transitions associated with young adulthood: gaining economic independence, partnering, having children, leaving the parental home, and in many cases gaining higher education or training.[7] Because the typical ages at which people engage these tasks change over time, so do the years that are considered part of young adulthood. Over the past few decades, many transitions that typically occurred in the early twenties or sooner began starting later and last-

5. Jensen and Arnett, "Going Global."
6. Jensen and Arnett, "Going Global."
7. Helen L. Bee and Barbara R. Bjorkland, *The Journey of Adulthood* (Hoboken: Prentice Hall, 2000); Marliss Buchmann, *The Script of Life in Modern Society: Entry into Adulthood in a Changing World* (Chicago: University of Chicago Press, 1989); Jensen and Arnett, "Going Global."

ing longer for many young adults. As an example, the average age of mothers when they gave birth in the United States has steadily risen from twenty-seven in 2007 to twenty-nine in 2018.[8]

Despite what trend analysis may suggest, there is no universal pattern for moving through life-stage transitions, nor is there a universal desire to engage in them.[9] This means that while using life stage as a marker of young adulthood is useful, it still comes with challenges. Further, whether one uses age or life stage to define young adulthood, each year new people enter while others move beyond the ages and stages, meaning young adulthood is populated by an ever-changing group of people for whom macrolevel environmental changes—such as a global pandemic or economic recession—can remake the landscape that determines the possibilities that are open to them.[10] Cohort models of young adulthood, with representative labels such as the millennial generation, attempt to address these factors. A drawback of the cohort model approach is that using a central external reference point makes it easy to assume that everyone in the cohort experienced or was influenced by their shared historical moment in the same way. Sorting out similarities from differences is a daunting and potentially unending endeavor.

The benefit of thinking about young adulthood through these different approaches (age, life stage, and cohort) is that it highlights some of the perplexities and challenges churches face when trying

8. "Average Age of Mother from the Births Data Summary Database," Sage Data, https://doi.org/10.6068/DP17B1319A2F08.

9. Dominika Winogrodzka and Izabela Grabowska, "(Dis)ordered Social Sequences of Mobile Young Adults: Spatial, Social and Return Mobilities," *Journal of Youth Studies* 25 (2022); Aurélie A. Mary, "Re-evaluating the Concept of Adulthood and the Framework of Transition," *Journal of Youth Studies* 17 (2014): 415–29; Paula Pustulka, Justyna Sarnowska, and Marta Buler, "Resources and Pace of Leaving Home among Young Adults in Poland," *Journal of Youth Studies* (2021): 1–17.

10. Richard A. Settersten Jr. et al., "Understanding the Effects of Covid-19 Through a Life Course Lens," *Advances in Life-Course Research* (2020).

to engage in ministry to and with young adults. Perhaps the most important point here is that defining young adulthood is more than a simple math problem or even a complex assessment of the degree of engagement with life-stage transitions or cohort membership, although these are important.

Young adulthood, with its rather fuzzy boundaries, also exists at the intersection of economic, civil, and religious realities, laws, and expectations.[11] For example, state laws determine the age at which one can marry, and legal and religious norms prescribe what constitutes an acceptable marriage partner. How young adults navigate these complexities has far-reaching and long-lasting consequences for their lives and the lives of their families and communities.[12] The church's role at this intersection can also have far-reaching and long-lasting consequences.[13]

Today's young adults make an excellent case study for the topic of how to live well in the transitions, as this cohort is navigating the pressure of traditional changes expected for their age and life stage while also traversing rough terrain unique to the times—the valley of the shadow of death amid the effects of a global pandemic;[14] a valley of broken dreams, as the gap between the rich and poor continues to widen; and the valley of broken promises, as the advances of technology and globalization degrade the environment and fail to generate enough decent work for all.[15] As today's young adults navigate these challenges, what do they require to live well? Is living well something only the privileged few can

11. Winogrodzka and Grabowska, "(Dis)ordered Social Sequences of Mobile Young Adults," 1–17.

12. Buchmann, *The Script of Life in Modern Society*; Jensen and Arnett, "Going Global."

13. Linda K. George, David B. Larson, Harold G. Koenig, and Michael E. McCullough, "Spirituality and Health: What We Know, What We Need to Know," *Journal of Social and Clinical Psychology* 19 (2000): 102–16.

14. Settersten, "Understanding the Effects of Covid-19 Through a Life Course Lens."

15. United Nations Secretary-General, "Progress towards the Sustainable

experience? Can it be experienced by everyone? Can it be experienced while in transition, or is it something that happens only when one has successfully navigated a transition and is safely on the other side? A closer look at living well may help us answer these questions.

Living Well

Living well is a personal and societal matter. While philosophers, theologians, psychologists, and sociologists continue to debate this matter extensively,[16] one of the most widely accepted and empirically supported definitions of living well is a subjective or personal assessment of one's happiness and satisfaction with life.[17] Critics have said this perspective promotes hedonism and narcissism through an excessive focus on self.[18] So an expanded theory of psychological well-being and mattering (which will be described below) is added to round out the definition of living well in this chapter.[19] Together these views address the individual and communal aspects of living well, as befits the church's commitment to the well-being of both individuals and communities.

Researchers have identified at least 197 variables related to well-being, with millions of unique combinations of these variables. Despite

Development Goals," United Nations Economic and Social Counsel, May 8, 2019, https://digitallibrary.un.org/record/3810131?ln=en.

16. Fallon R. Goodman, David J. Disabato, Todd B. Kashdan, and Scott B. Kauffman, "Measuring Well-Being: A Comparison of Subjective Well-Being and PERMA," *The Journal of Positive Psychology* 13, no. 4 (2018): 321–32; Carol D. Ryff, "Psychological Well-Being in Adult Life," *Current Directions in Psychological Science* 4 (1995): 99–104.

17. Ed Diener, Robert A. Emmons, Randy J. Larsen, and Sharon Griffin, "The Satisfaction with Life Scale," *Journal of Personality Assessment* 49 (1985): 71–75; Goodman et al., "Measuring Well-Being."

18. Ryff, "Psychological Well-Being in Adult Life."

19. Isaac Prilleltensky, "Mattering at the Intersection of Psychology, Philosophy, and Politics," *American Journal of Community Psychology* 65 (2020): 16–34.

this daunting situation, most research fortunately and consistently converges on two factors of well-being: happiness and satisfaction with life.[20] From this vantage point, living well is defined simply as the degree to which one experiences happiness and satisfaction in life. What leads to these experiences varies by person, but it typically involves the fulfillment of basic human needs for existence, relatedness, and growth.[21] McClelland conceptualized relatedness and growth as affiliation with others, power, and achievement.[22] Viktor Frankl, who survived the Nazi concentration and extermination camps, proposed that even when these most basic needs cannot be met, there is one all-pervasive need left to constitute a well-lived life: the need for meaning. Frankl argues persuasively in his short and powerful book, *Man's Search for Meaning*, that a person can still feel a measure of happiness and satisfaction with life if they know that their life has meaning.[23]

Frankl's view notwithstanding, critics of subjective well-being suggest it focuses too much attention on the self. Whether living well is defined in terms of individual need for existence, relatedness, growth, or meaning, even Hitler's soldiers could be said to have been living well.[24] For moral and ethical reasons, then, let's explore additional definitions. Carol Ryff, one of the strongest critics of the hedonic view of living well, suggests that striving to become one's best

20. Goodman et al., "Measuring Well-Being," 321–32.

21. Clayton P. Aldefer, *Existence, Relatedness, and Growth: Human Needs in Organizational Settings* (New York: Free Press, 1972); Roy F. Baumeister and Mark R. Leary, "The Need to Belong: Desire for Interpersonal Attachments as a Fundamental Human Motivation," *Psychological Bulletin* 117, no. 3 (1995): 497; Diener et al., "The Satisfaction with Life Scale"; Abraham H. Maslow, *Motivation and Personality* (New York: Harper & Row, 1954).

22. David C. McClelland, *The Achieving Society* (New York: Van Nostrand, 1961).

23. Viktor E. Frankl, *Man's Search for Meaning* (New York: Simon & Schuster, 1985).

24. Ryan D. Duffy, Bryan J. Dik, Richard P. Douglass, Jessica W. England, and Brandon L. Velez, "Work as a Calling: A Theoretical Model," *Journal of Counseling Psychology* 65, no. 4 (2018): 423–39.

self is what constitutes living well. Her well-being model contains six key elements: self-acceptance, positive relations with other people, autonomy, environmental mastery, purpose in life, and personal growth.[25] Ryff admits that this wider view was built from a Western vantage point and suggests that while all of the elements matter, each may be valued at different degrees depending on one's culture or personality. She also suggests that some may be harder to attain than others depending on one's economic and social circumstances.

Community psychologist Isaac Prilleltensky goes even further to suggest that it is not enough to have a holistic perspective of living well; he says there must be equal balance between "feeling valued and adding value."[26] A good example of this is the experience Pivot NW Research churches had with young adults in leadership. As will be explained further in the following chapter, churches found that a balance of autonomy and support allowed young adult leaders to take ownership and add value while still feeling valued and supported. This balance requires a sufficiently equitable distribution of goods and power in a group for everyone to be able to add value in equal measure. It is this ability to *create* value, not just to *be* valued, that Prilleltensky argues makes all the difference in a person's psychological and subjective well-being. Interestingly, this model that Prilleltensky calls *mattering* deals with the material aspects of living well better than many others.

Subjective models of living well do not ignore material well-being but subsume it as a personal assessment under life satisfaction. Liberation theologians astutely point out that anything causing a person to feel satisfied with an unfair distribution of wealth, be it social capital or material goods, cannot be called good.[27] This perspective calls the church to think beyond simply recognizing others as made in the

25. Ryff, "Psychological Well-Being in Adult Life," 101.

26. Prilleltensky, "Mattering at the Intersection of Psychology, Philosophy, and Politics," 17.

27. Miguel A. De La Torre, *Reading the Bible from the Margins* (Maryknoll, NY: Orbis Books, 2002).

image of God and therefore valuable and worthy of love or charity. It calls on a fundamental redistribution of power so that everyone can live out their God-given call to have a prosocial impact. This radical vision is challenging in today's society, where entrenched capital markets attract the most investment and where hierarchical pay practices inhibit workers' access to and enjoyment of the fruits of their labor. Limited access to the fruits of their labor, including economic and social capital, in turn inhibits workers from mattering in civic and social arenas where they would otherwise invest, if they had the opportunity. Mattering, according to Prilleltensky, requires being seen as a person of dignity and worth as well as being able to influence the direction and outcomes of the institutions that govern our lives.

One last vision rounds out the picture of what it means to live well. Galatians 5:22–23 proposes nine fruits of the Spirit (love, joy, peace, patience, kindness, generosity, faithfulness, gentleness, and self-control) as marks, if not the whole sum and substance, of living well. Only when taken together with the greatest commandment to love God and the second greatest to love others as oneself (Matt. 22:37–39) can self-love, as represented in measures of subjective well-being, enter the picture safely. Before we turn our attention to transitions, it is important to dive a little deeper into four facets of well-being—specifically happiness, life satisfaction, personal growth, and prosocial impact. What we learn from this dive may help us at least survive and perhaps thrive in life's transitions and beyond.

Researchers sometimes measure happiness as the ratio of positive to negative emotions that a person experiences.[28] At first, this seemed strange to me, as I had always envisioned positive and negative emotions as opposite ends of a continuum. It came as a great relief to learn that they are in fact separate dimensions,[29] which means that one can

28. Diener et al., "The Satisfaction with Life Scale"; Goodman et al., "Measuring Well-Being."
29. Adam A. Augustine and Randy J. Larsen, "Personality, Affect, and

indeed experience joy in the midst of sorrow, or peace in the midst of pain, as sorrow and pain seem to be built into the marrow of this life. Personality researchers have found that some people have a natural tendency to experience a lot of positive emotions and fewer negative emotions. Others tend to experience a lot of negative emotions and fewer positive ones. Yet others have the tendency to experience a lot of emotions, both positive and negative, while others experience fewer of both. Personality is a starting point for happiness but not the end point. Situations and other people call forth emotions in us,[30] and so it is possible to increase positive feelings. While some people may need more positive boosting than others to tip the scale, there is hope for happiness.

While happiness is a feeling, life satisfaction is a thought or a cognitive assessment of our situation in life.[31] This assessment occurs at the intersection of our self and society. We learn what our life should be like by observing the people around us and modeling our behavior accordingly. As we grow up, however, our personal agency or free will, coupled with our thinking abilities, allows us to change the script and to shape our own lives with purpose and meaning.[32] In this way, life satisfaction and personal growth are intertwined. Interestingly, the tenth commandment in the Old Testament—paraphrased as "You should not covet what your neighbor has"—is juxtaposed with a multibillion-dollar marketing industry that influences us to do just that. This reminds us that what we think about will influence how

Affect Regulation," in *APA Handbook of Personality and Social Psychology*, vol. 4, *Personality Processes and Individual Differences*, ed. M. Mikulincer, P. R. Shaver, and L. M. Cooper (2015), 147–65.

30. Yuichi Shoda, Nicole L. Wilson, Donna D. Whitsett, Jenna Lee-Dussud, and Vivian Zayas, "The Person as a Cognitive-Affective Processing System: Quantitative Ideography as an Integral Component of Cumulative Science," in *APA Handbook of Personality and Social Psychology*, 4:491–513.

31. Diener et al., "The Satisfaction with Life Scale," 71–75.

32. Albert Bandura, *Social Foundations of Thought and Action: A Social Cognitive Theory* (Englewood Cliffs, NJ: Prentice-Hall, 1986).

satisfied we are with our lives and motivate our actions accordingly (Exod. 20:17; Prov. 23:7).

Speaking of action, prosocial impact, or doing good for the benefit of others, has been found to have a positive impact on life satisfaction and how people feel about themselves and their work.[33] Not only that, experiencing action with others is a potent force for creating social support and bonding. Pivot NW Research participants reported that some of the strongest bonds between young adults or or between them and others were forged while engaging together in social justice marches, serving community needs, or helping one another with Bible studies and spiritual retreats.

What this brief but nuanced deeper dive shows us is that living well involves feelings, thoughts, and actions, all three of which provide pathways or intervention opportunities for living better. This encouraging picture of living well will frame the following discussion of transitions and their relationship with living well.

Transitions

A popular image used in life-stage research is that of two clocks to describe the drivers of transition in young adulthood.[34] The first is the biological clock that marks time based on physical needs and capabilities. The second is the social clock representing cultural expectations and norms. Together, these clocks put pressure on people to engage in and complete major life transitions. For young adults, these often include three major life tasks: obtaining economic sufficiency, finding

33. Adam M. Grant and Sabine Sonnentag, "Doing Good Buffers against Feeling Bad: Prosocial Impact Compensates for Negative Task and Self-Evaluations," *Organizational Behavior and Human Decision Processes* 111, no. 1 (2010): 13.

34. Bee and Bjorkland, *The Journey of Adulthood*; Ceri Wilson and Jennifer Stock, "The Impact of Living with Long-Term Conditions in Young Adulthood on Mental Health and Identity: What Can Help?," *Health Expect* 22 (2019): 1111–21; Winogrodzka and Grabowska, "(Dis)ordered Social Sequences of Mobile Young Adults," 1–17.

partners, and having children. In Western countries especially, the pressure can be very strong to start, if not complete, these transitions before the age of thirty.[35] Two more transitions support and enable these, materially or symbolically: leaving the parental home and pursuing advanced education or training.[36] In the United States, living independently of parents and attending college or university often are seen as valuable transitions in their own right. Taken together or separately, each of these transitions has far-reaching and long-lasting consequences for young adults, their families, and their communities.[37]

Communities today are broader than ever as evolving technology, increasing mobility, and globalization transform societies, cultures, and even biological possibilities.[38] Life-stage transitions that may have occurred more predictably for many during the industrial era in the West are less sequential and more fluid in the postindustrial era. While the use of the word "clock" makes it seem as if life-stage transitions were once unidirectional and evenly paced, it is important to note that there has always been a degree of variety in both the speed and direction of life changes, with attendant consequences.[39] Transitions may be smooth and congruent with existing beliefs and values, supported by adequate resources. They also can occur at a crisis pace or turbulently over a long period of time with or without adequate physical, emotional, and social resources.[40]

35. Bee and Bjorkland, *The Journey of Adulthood*; Buchmann, *The Script of Life in Modern Society*.

36. Arnett, "Emerging Adulthood," 469–80.

37. Buchmann, *The Script of Life in Modern Society*; Jensen and Arnett, "Going Global."

38. Pustulka, Sarnowska, and Buler, "Resources and Pace of Leaving Home Among Young Adults in Poland," 1–17.

39. Roger Avery, Frances Goldscheider, and Alden Speare Jr., "Feathered Nest/Gilded Cage: Parental Income and Leaving Home in the Transition to Adulthood," *Demography* 29, no. 3 (1992): 375–88.

40. Pustulka, Sarnowska, and Buler, "Resources and Pace of Leaving Home among Young Adults in Poland," 1–17.

It is important to remember that young adulthood—with its rather fuzzy boundaries, ticking clocks, and increasingly mobile character—exists at the intersection of economic, civil, and religious realities, laws, and expectations.[41] It bears repeating that how young adults navigate these complexities has far-reaching and long-lasting consequences for their lives and the lives of their families and communities. While the goal of life-stage transitions for societies is to perpetuate the society and ensure its survival and continuity, for individuals transitions are pathways for fulfilling personal wants and needs.[42] Thinking of transitions from the perspective of biological and social clocks helps us understand why transitions in young adulthood are not just important, but also experienced as urgent.

As helpful as the clock image may be, thinking of transitions as paths provides even more nuance and possibility for understanding the role of transitions in our lives.[43] While clocks create pressure, paths provide possibility. Social customs, laws, and norms provide predetermined pathways for living well. Developed over time and understood as the collective direction of a culture, transition paths, carved deep over decades or even centuries of repeated use, are seen as time-tested and culturally validated means to valued ends. Parents wanting grandchildren highlight having children as fulfillment. Books and movies provide pervasive reminders of the importance of finding "the one" partner who will give meaning and purpose to life. And in a capitalist economy, the idea that economic self-sufficiency is equal to happiness is so deeply ingrained that we almost take it for granted. For many, however, accepting these ideas means that they may spend a decade or more of their lives in pursuit of these ideals and, despite their best efforts, may never arrive.[44]

41. Winogrodzka and Grabowska, "(Dis)ordered Social Sequences of Mobile Young Adults."

42. Bee and Bjorkland, *The Journey of Adulthood.*

43. Winogrodzka and Grabowska, "(Dis)ordered Social Sequences of Mobile Young Adults."

44. Mary, "Re-evaluating the Concept of Adulthood and the Frame-

What about the other two transitions that are often associated with young adulthood? Universities promise that an education will lead to a better quality of life. Realtors and apartment marketers highlight that living in a particular place will result in greater joy. Perhaps there is some truth to all the hype, and at the end of each of these transition paths awaits a pot of gold or at least a moment of pleasure. The aim of this chapter is not to argue with cultural claims that transitions can lead to living well. Instead, the goal is to ask, *What about the transition period itself?* What happens when a person is in process, for a little while or for a lifetime? What happens when a clock breaks and biology lets us down? Or what happens when cultural constraints break us because we don't fit the mold? When the end of a transition path takes a long time to reach, or even when it is out of reach or undesired, are we prevented from living well?

While life-stage transitions matter, they are not the whole of young adulthood. There are other relationships to be built and maintained, volunteer work and housework to do, political choices to make, and more. If transitions are seen not as pathways *to* a life well lived, but rather opportunities *for* living well in the moment, they become more hopeful and perhaps more manageable. Here we come full circle to what constitutes well-being and which ways we can experience it. In 1977, Michael Fordyce suggested that instead of hoping for happiness as a byproduct of other things, we can focus on improving it directly. He came up with a fourteen-step plan that included educating people about happiness and having them think about it and then attempt specific exercises to boost it with good results.[45] Perhaps this is possible for young adults in transition. If someone directly seeks to love others, experience joy, cultivate peace, exhibit patience, practice

work of Transition"; Pustulka, Sarnowska, and Buler, "Resources and Pace of Leaving Home among Young Adults in Poland"; Wilson and Stock, "The Impact of Living with Long-Term Conditions in Young Adulthood on Mental Health and Identity."

45. M. W. Fordyce, "A Program to Increase Happiness: Further Studies," *Journal of Counseling Psychology* 30, no. 4 (1983): 483–98.

kindness, goodness, faithfulness, gentleness, and self-control, does this mean that they are in fact experiencing what it means to live well? Yes and no. Psychologists tell us it's not enough to add value; we also need to experience being valued. Both-and.

Each day requires decisions that have the potential to change our lives in unforeseen ways. The fact that we spend a lot of our life in transition is bad news if we believe that living well is the result of successfully completing desired or sometimes undesired transitions. The fact that we spend a lot of our life in transition is good news if we believe that every transition—the big life-stage ones and all the others as well—is a pathway for living well. Within the transition, within the process of change itself, are access points for living well, for directly accessing joy, life satisfaction, purpose, and mattering. We don't have to wait to experience abundant life (John 10:10). The conditions are available even in the midst of life's transitions.

It has been said that life is like a trapeze act; it involves swinging and letting go of what came before and then straining to grasp what is coming next. Yet we live often in the space of time between what we are letting go of and what we are straining for—hanging in the air without a net to catch us. In a circus, such moments of tension are spellbinding, but in life these moments are times of transitions that we all inevitability face in quiet ways. This is what it is like to be a young adult in our world today—letting go of the past and straining for an unknown future.

The clocks are ticking, it is true. The pressures are real, and we should never underestimate the toll they can take on young adults or people of any age or life stage. Researchers who study change have observed that the change curve and the grief curve mirror each other to a startling degree.[46] This suggests that no matter how joyous or smooth a transition may seem, there is a process of letting go involved that can invoke grief, even when the transition was highly desired. This is

46. Elisabeth Kübler-Ross Foundation, "Kübler-Ross Change Curve," Elisabeth Kübler-Ross Foundation website, 2022. https://www.ekrfounda tion.org/5-stages-of-grief/change-curve/.

what makes it a transition rather than simply an addition. The trapeze image seen above is one often used to represent transition. Whether one is well prepared to launch from one swinging bar to the next or is still learning how to fly, whether the next trapeze bar swings smoothly into place or wildly in a crosswind, there is a moment between what was and what will be when uncertainty seeks faith. Danaan Parry describes this as a moment of transformation. For those seeking faith, the church can be a wonderful resource for living well.[47]

A staff member at a Seattle church asked a question many church workers might relate to: "How do I exist in that space but also as part of this staff, this team of pastors? In our church context, how do we sort of be intentional to move people closer to the gospel, fully knowing that this is a season? This is going to be a constantly changing thing." As stated at the beginning of this chapter, the Christian church has long considered itself as a place of hope and resources for living well, yet young adults are increasingly turning elsewhere to find support for navigating life.[48] Perhaps one clue as to why this is so can be found in the similarities between the change curve and the grief curve that were mentioned earlier. Avoiding hurt and conserving energy were key reasons young adults gave for not connecting to churches. These are also reasons older church members gave for waiting to see how often young adults would come back before investing in relationships with them. It is important to recognize this in today's highly mobile society, in which pressures come from every angle. Even though there is great opportunity for personal growth and transformation when people in different stages of life connect with each other, there is also the potential for grief and hurt. For churches willing to embrace the challenge, the invitation to lean into this hurt and discomfort for the sake of young adults is a beckoning call. Two of the most compelling questions asked by Pivot NW Research participants and researchers, who were also young adults,

---

47. D. Parry, *Warriors of the Heart* (Kalaheo, HI: The Earthstewards Network, 2009).

48. Killen and Silk, *Religion and Public Life in the Pacific Northwest.*

were *Can the church become a transition station, and does it want to be?* To what degree is it ready to invest in people who will only be around for a season or less?

Pivot Northwest participants asked many questions about what it might mean to intentionally occupy the space of uncertainty and transition with young adults. What would it look like for churches to value young adults to the extent that they give them opportunities to lead and develop others, even when they are just passing through? Does it require changing expectations about things like membership and belonging? Would they benefit from changing expectations about how and when people connect to a church building or services? It certainly requires grappling with the compelling issues of the day like technology, mobility, and globalization, not as intruding forces that are erasing cherished traditions but as present realities that young adults cannot avoid. It also means looking at the ways in which mattering has been denied to people in the past and changing structures or policies that keep people from being able to give as much as they receive. These thoughtful questions and ideas are closely aligned with the research on living well. Based on the living well research, there are many ways the church can be a resource station for young adults coping with the challenges and uncertainties in their lives.

Supporting Young Adults in Transition

What transitions are the young adults in your church or your community coping with? Borrowing imagery from Psalm 23, here are some ways the church can respond.

- *Coping through the valley of the shadow of death*: Help young adults see the purpose and meaning of their lives despite all the cultural voices that would deny their dignity.
- *Coping through the valley of broken dreams*: Help young adults find happiness in the moment and provide an antidote to the pressure to complete transitions in order to experience happiness.

- *Coping through the valley of broken promises*: Transfer power to young adults, enabling them to shape the future of the church and to make a difference in the lives of others using the church's wealth and resources.

In addition to these valuable cognitive, emotional, and material resources, the church also has access to spiritual resources that can make a difference. Linda George and her fellow researchers reviewed numerous studies on the impact of religious participation and beliefs and found that positive religious coping, described as faith in a God who personally loves and cares for oneself, was related to better health outcomes and well-being.[49] Given the value of positive religious coping as a resource for living well, it may be helpful to explore it in more depth.

Religious Coping as a Valuable Resource for Living Well

Religious coping can be conceived of as positive or negative.[50] At the heart of religious coping is one's view of God as either forgiving or punitive. Both viewpoints can motivate a person to try harder and persist longer in times of transition; hence, they are both considered coping mechanisms. Those with the more positive view of God, however, reported better psychological outcomes and greater happiness than those with a more negative view of God. In fact, those who reported a greater reliance on negative religious coping had worse psychological outcomes than those who used no religious coping at all.

Rather than attributing religious coping to a person and making it a dispositional matter, some scholars have conceptualized religious

49. George , Larson, Koenig, and McCullough, "Spirituality and Health," 102–16.

50. Kenneth I. Pargament, "The Bitter and the Sweet: An Evaluation of the Costs and Benefits of Religiousness," *Psychological Inquiry* 13 (2002): 168–81.

coping as a resource external to the person. In this light the church, especially when operating as a transition station, can be seen as a resource-rich site with much to offer young adults. Providing young adults with a perspective of God as merciful, personal, and caring gives them a resource to draw upon in times of transition to help them cope with difficult circumstances. A study on the impact of spiritual support, defined as "perceived support from God,"[51] found that for young adults experiencing high levels of stress, spiritual support did indeed have a strong positive impact on well-being over and above social support from friends and family. Recognizing that not all forms of religious coping result in positive psychological outcomes is important, however. Negative religious coping, or punitive appraisals and perspectives of God, can cause more psychological harm than good, while warm, personal, and loving appraisals and perspectives can buffer the stress of transition. This discussion of spiritual support leads to the conclusion of this chapter and a look back over key takeaways from Pivot NW Research and other research highlighted in this chapter.

Conclusion

Young adulthood is a time of multiple simultaneous high-stakes transitions that create tremendous stress for young adults. Based in the research on living well, there are several ways the church can help young adults not only survive but thrive in the transitions of life. First, going directly for happiness and joy and engaging in activities that boost these can help to buffer the stress of change. Second, providing resources and support for finding meaning and purpose in God rather than in the transitions held up by society as normal and expected can provide psychological salve in the midst of a painful world—especially

51. Kenneth I. Maton, "The Stress-Buffering Role of Spiritual Support: Cross-Sectional and Prospective Investigations," *Journal for the Scientific Study of Religion* 28 (1989): 310–32.

when those transitions are not working out or have failed. Third, re-distributing power and physical resources to young adults so they can influence the shape and direction of their own lives and the institutions through which they live them is an act of faith and hope. This act perhaps holds the greatest promise for changing the trajectory of the Christian church from dwindling in importance and relevance in the lives of young adults to growing in importance and impact.

Churches that want to be transition stations can embrace all or some of these ideas. As each cohort of young adults navigates the unique circumstances of its time as well as the biological and social clocks that constrain and enable those young adults, the church has a special role in contributing to religious coping that, when positive in nature, has been shown to make a difference. As young adults navigate the transitions of life, they become examples of what is possible and sources of renewable energy and excitement as they invite the next generation of transition-station attendants into the work and life of the church. If the church chooses to act as a resource station—helping young adults experience joy, meaning, and mattering even through transition—not only will the lives of young adults be improved, but so will the life of the whole church.

Chapter Reflection Questions

1. Think of young adults (or if you are a young adult, then peers) that you know and catalogue the transitions they are going through. Now consider your own situation at their age. What are the similarities and differences?

2. How have you received value from having a prosocial impact in your community or church?

3. Have you ever experienced the generosity or protection of someone during a difficult transition? Have you ever offered that to someone else?

4. While clocks create pressure, paths provide possibility. Social customs, laws, and norms provide predetermined pathways for

living well. Consider which clocks and pathways you have encountered and how they hindered or helped you?

5. What does it mean to you and your church to live well in the transitions of life?

6. How can your church help young adults live well in those transitions?

7. What support can you provide to young adults while they are with you?

8. What struggles do you anticipate as you connect with a highly transient population?

5

Identified Not Developed

Young Adults in Leadership

MACKENZIE HARRIS

We must take seriously the pain of those who protest for
justice . . . it means moving in the world with empathy
not entitlement. Instead of moving through the world as
if we are entitled to life, liberty and happiness because of
who we are, where we are born, or what we look like—as
if somehow, we are special while others are not—we are to
move through the world with empathy. This means we are
to allow ourselves to feel the suffering, the heartache, the
hunger of others for life, liberty and happiness—for justice.

—Rev. Dr. Kelly Brown Douglas,
"To Do Justice for Jordan Davis"

In the first five years of our work with young adults and churches, we
had a number of speakers do presentations about their fields of inquiry,
how young adulthood intersected those fields, and what the outcomes
were for those interactions. In what we heard from diversity, equity,
and inclusion professionals; artists; musicians; storytellers; and min-

istry workers in ethnically diverse contexts, it became clear that young adults could often receive accolades and responsibility in secular situations, but when it came to churches, young adults were often infantilized, patronized, and minimized. Even when young adults were able to lead, people often feared that they would lead in the wrong direction. Some churches believed that young adults weren't mature, tested, and integrated enough to be leaders. This often was code for them not being assimilated, indoctrinated, or resigned to caretaking the projects and priorities of the older generations.

One particular phrase from the Reverend Leroy Barber caught our attention and imagination. He said, "The church needs to focus on identifying leaders, not developing them!" Barber said this in the context of helping the church to empower leaders who are already working in communities of color rather than airdropping in leaders who are foreign to the neighborhood cultural context, but the idea has merit beyond the context of urban multicultural mission work. In most contexts, the church should be asking itself, *What is the appropriate way to engage young adults so that they feel empowered and not abandoned, overworked, underresourced, or untrusted?*

Leadership identification and subsequent empowerment are built on trust, faith, and relationships that come out of mutual commitment. While our churches often described taking a leap of faith when they empowered young adults in their congregations, these leaps of faith were rewarded with relationships built, trust built, and increased faith in the ability of young adults to step into positions of power.

This chapter addresses the importance of having young adults in leadership, and it discusses the need for and struggles of commitment between the three main constituencies involved in this arrangement—the pastoral staff, the young adults, and the larger congregation.

Pastoral Commitment to Young Adult Groups

During our five-year study, we witnessed constant negotiations between young adult innovation teams and the larger congregational leadership structure. Those in senior leadership roles often struggled while learning how to engage with young adult leaders or leadership teams. Often, pastors or other senior leaders felt that their roles were unclear when it came to supporting young adult leaders. Should they have a hand in decision-making, or should they leave it all in the young adults' hands? Do they attend young adult events, providing hands-on support, or do they maintain some distance and simply act as consultants when their young adult leaders look for advice? These questions were not unique to new young adult ministries; long-established and fledgling programs alike dealt with these questions.

A common question for churches working to amplify young adult voices is about how much time the pastors should allocate to those ministries. Often pastoral attention is recognized as the most valuable possession a church has to offer both its members and the community outside of the building. The question of whether to hire an additional staff person to lead a new ministry and the return on investment of that decision is a major consideration.

Many churches choose either close oversight verging on micromanagement or, at the other end of the spectrum, distant oversight verging on abandonment. However, just as in parenting, employee supervision, and many similar tasks that require intergenerational interaction, the best course often lies somewhere in between. The complexity is increased by not just the quantity of oversight, but also the quality of it. There is a difference between the involvement of an associate pastor or elder and that of the senior or lead pastor, especially as the size of the church and various demands on senior leaders' time grow. Our colleagues doing this work with predominantly Lutheran congregations in the Twin Cities through Augsburg University put it best when they said that pastors can be one of the biggest drivers to successfully elevating the stories of young adults in their congregation by being actively involved or mercifully absent from the process. On the other hand, they can be the biggest obstacles by being overly controlling of the processes, or by being unwilling or unable to remove obstacles for the group because of their lack of investment.

With so many possible approaches and outcomes just from the involvement, or lack thereof, by the senior pastor, one can imagine how infinitely more complicated it gets with each additional person who is asked or expected to be involved and pull a portion of the load.

Despite the challenges of stewarding fruitful young adult ministries, there are many tactics that have worked well for churches.

At one of the churches with which we partnered three young adults were looking to create an intentional faith-based community for their age group. The two head pastors invited these young adults over for dinner to discuss their ideas for the group, serving them food and listening intently. The pastors initially wanted to provide direction to this young adult team, but after listening, they stepped back and asked how they could offer support and be most helpful. The young adult leaders wanted their pastors' advice and support, but they really wanted to steer the ship on their own. The pastors respected that wish, and the relationship that formed between them became one of mentorship and mutual respect rather than one of hierarchy and power. With mentorship and shared power as the foundation of the interaction between church leadership and young adult ministry leadership, the group flourished.

This story taught us that young adult ministries can exist within churches while still being their own entities. For a young adult group to be successful, establishing good rapport and a high level of trust between the two leadership groups is vital to reaching the greatest possible number of young adults. A strong partnership between senior church leaders and young adult leadership is important, but allowing the young adults to own their ministries provides space that fosters growth and love for the young adults in their local communities, which often leads the young adults to become more involved in their churches on Sundays. Some mentioned leading worship or preaching at church, feeling confident enough to do so because they knew their young adult group friends would be cheering them on from the front pews.

Allowing young adults to really *share* ownership of the decisions made within their young adult communities is important. There seems to be a fine balance when considering the degree of involvement the congregation assumes in a resident young adult ministry. Some pastors and church leadership teams met often with the young adult leadership groups. This was successful so long as the church leaders gave the young adult leadership teams the final say in determining which direction to move. Support from the church leadership was valuable and built a sense of confidence in the young adult leaders, but too much involvement was not as beneficial. Young adults felt more secure about owning their decisions when they felt support from the church even if their ideas failed.

The Challenge of Young Adult Commitment

If the church can commit pastoral time, church council oversight, financial support, and maybe some intergenerational leadership, then the big question is whether young adults will value all that effort and show up to help create the community. Like the question in the movie *Field of Dreams*, the church may ask, "If we build it, will they come?" Yes and no. A perpetual challenge for young adult leadership in the church is young adult commitment. With what can seem like mountains of other problems in their lives, sometimes young adults do not make church a priority, much less leadership in the church. As with interpersonal relationships, one side can give more than the other, leaving the giving side (often the church) feeling exhausted. Churches can become tired of investing in young adults when they do not feel as if the effort is being reciprocated. Tension arises when expectations of commitment to the church are misaligned with young adult relationship priorities. Churches want to help young adults solve their problems (which is a bid for intimacy and commitment); young adults feel as though they do not have enough time to give to a relationship with the church. It can feel like a big risk to pour time into a church for young adults who already feel that they do not have time to solve their own problems. Similarly, the young adult leadership teams experienced some burnout and fatigue when it came to pouring time and effort into their young adult communities.

One could call this a scarcity spiral. Momentum or critical mass for sustaining a young adult group can also be likened to a three-legged stool. If in any one leg (young adult leadership, young adult excitement and buy-in, church resourcing and intergenerational support) seems to be short, then no amount of overcorrection will make the surface flat.

Where young adults craving a faith community were matched with efforts by intergenerational support and leadership, our young adult leaders who were planning events and meetings for their young adult communities would at times voice discouragement about their peers' priorities. As young adult leaders became a bit more discouraged, their will to continue pouring energy into these groups lessened with time. At times it felt like observing a chicken or the egg conundrum; young adults need these young adult faith communities to receive support through challenges, but committing to the young adult faith communities takes precious time away from solving some of those challenges.

Which ought to be prioritized: young adults' need for a supportive faith community to aid them in life, or their need to grapple with pressures that they face as they go through so many transitions—which can, hopefully, free up time later for community? It is hard to identify the inception or culmination of this loop. Nevertheless, when this replays in young adults' minds, typically the problems that they're facing end up winning the battle for time investment. Time is a limited resource; young adults are overwhelmed by the number of commitments they have, and adding one more to their plate may not be feasible.

As trite and perhaps unsatisfactory as it might seem, "Come to me, all you that are weary and are carrying heavy burdens, and I will give you rest" (Matt. 11:28) expresses probably one of the main ways to cultivate a committed and grace-filled young adult community. Or in the words of Pacific Northwest prophet Kurt Cobain, "Come as you are." This reflects the ethos we have learned by watching young adults gather—that the gathering is the first, most important step, and they will figure out the rest if they feel safe, supported, and encouraged. The gathering itself, even if it feels burdensome, becomes the hurdle, and young adults will often find rest, will feel seen, and will feel more empowered for having jumped it.

Young Adult Leadership Commitment

As explained in the previous chapter, young adulthood is filled with transitions—many of which may draw young adults away from particular faith communities for short or extended periods of time. The first step in managing these challenges is accepting that transition is a natural part of young adulthood. It isn't necessarily a poor reflection on your community or ministries; it's just a reality of life. In fact, an ungraceful approach to this is often a surefire way to discourage young adults from returning to communities after major life transitions.

Despite that reality, there are ways to mitigate the upheaval and disconnection that can arise as young adults' lives and priorities shift.

One way is having young adult leaders waiting in the wings, ready to step in when someone needs to step back from their leadership responsibilities. This allows for smoother transitions from one person to the next. As we will discuss, mentoring paired with succession planning helps even more. Simply put, it's the cultivation of a deep bench for leadership.

Young adult leaders who support other young adults will most likely need to step away at times. Having a diverse group of young people in your young adult groups is vital for sustainability. Allowing people to become as involved as they would like and to get exposure to leading at their pace and in their style helps build a leadership bench. Having people ready to tag in when someone has to tag out will ensure that the group does not miss a beat, even if someone needs to step back for a longer period of time.

Young adults are often members of a small population that experiences high transiency and high demands on time from various commitments, and because of this the church can easily assume young adults have little care for participating in leadership. This may not be the case, however, as many young adults have an eagerness and energy for leadership that many older adults lack. Another way to say that is: What young adults lack in stability and consistency they can often make up for with intensity, creativity, and energy. Young adults are formed by contemporary problems and will be better versed in contemporary solutions than older adults whose core formation will be dated to older problems and their respective reactions. It's important for older members of congregations to see that a lack of attention to their priorities by young adults doesn't equal a lack of care for intergenerational problems or a desire to avoid leadership responsibilities. It is just a different set of lenses through which problems are seen.

As with any marginalized group, it is easy for the majority to see the flaws of the minority quite clearly while minimizing the flaws of the majority. It's important for older adults in our churches to consider the power of flipping that tendency on its head so that the strengths of young adults are highlighted when considering how to equip and encourage them.

Mentorship Reinforcing Mutual Commitment

If having more young adult leaders ready to take on responsibility is key to navigating young adult transience, the question then becomes, *How do churches support young adults as they prepare for leadership roles?*

An important part of helping young adults feel comfortable stepping into positions of leadership is mentorship. Mentorship can be between an elder and someone of a younger generation, or even someone with a little more experience and someone with less experience in a particular area. Young adults crave strong mentoring relationships to seek wise counsel and look for guidance. This does not replace peer relationships but seems to recognize that peers share common questions and a lack of answers. While peer relationships are often great for empathy due to common experience, there is also a spiritual need for hope for the future, something that is embodied by older mentors who have weathered their own adversity. Empathy is irreplaceable in every relationship of the young adult experience. But just like a dissonant chord, the resolution of empathy into hope is an important and biblical relational evolution.

Research has shown us that the key factor between being able to identify one's calling and actually living out that calling is having a mentor there to support one's pursuit of that calling.[1] We believe that this kind of relationship is vital for young adults who want to live purpose-driven lives, especially when their mentors share the same spiritual backgrounds.

Mentoring relationships need to be approached thoughtfully, as we discovered these relationships can just as easily harm as help. Relationships are hard. Intergenerational relationships can be even harder. Building a trusted mentoring relationship is difficult when values, cultural touchpoints, and vitality aren't shared, and when mentors do not clearly understand that they will grow just as much in the process as their mentees. This is why we have focused on the practice of *reverse mentorship*.

Reverse mentorship is "an inverted relationship, pairing junior workers to help more experienced leaders acquire new learning,"[2] and it has the ability to build bridges across the generational divide.[3] Church leaders, often from older generations than the leaders of their

---

1. Kyle Ehrhardt and Ellen Ensher, "Perceiving a Calling, Living a Calling, and Calling Outcomes: How Mentoring Matters," *Journal of Counseling Psychology* 68, no. 2 (2021): 168.

2. Sanghamitra Chaudhuri and Rajashi Ghosh, "Reverse Mentoring: A Social Exchange Tool for Keeping the Boomers Engaged and Millennials Committed," *Human Resource Development Review* 11, no. 1 (2012): 55–76.

3. Ian Browne, "Exploring Reverse Mentoring: 'Win-Win' Relationships

young adult groups, have had a hard time knowing how to support young adults. Often, this springs from fear of getting it wrong or maybe a fear of rejection—two very possible outcomes. A reverse mentoring approach helps mitigate these fears since it is based on positivity, respect, and a desire to learn from one another.

One tack that can be taken is an actual covenant with ground rules or another structured set of interactions to build trust. These reverse mentoring relationships can help members of the younger generation deepen self-awareness, learn more about themselves, feel free from outside observation and judgment, and increase their idea generation. Members of the older generation can gain a deeper sense of self, accept their deficiencies, and assess their aspirations and vulnerabilities, also without fear of outside judgement.[4]

In the context of our research and observation, this type of relationship could look like a pastor and a young adult leadership team member meeting up for coffee or having dinner at the pastor's house once a month to chat about struggles and wins. Pastors who did this were able to remain connected to the young adult ministry without overstepping power boundaries, and young adult leaders felt well supported. The pastors usually learned a lot about themselves and the young adults' perspective, creating a connection point that was safe for both parties.

Peer Mentoring

Another form of mentoring is peer mentoring, having the young adult leaders support and mentor each other. When peers coach and mentor each other, they can build up one another's self-efficacy, support one another, and develop identities that resonate with their own personal experiences. These relationships often transcend the

in the Multi-generational Workplace," *International Journal of Evidence Based Coaching and Mentoring* 15 (2021): 246–59.

4. Browne, "Exploring Reverse Mentoring," 246–59.

confinements of culture, gender, race, or ability status.[5] Benefits of the peer mentoring relationship include feeling an increased sense of belonging, creating a support network, and increasing access to advice and resources.[6]

We see tremendous value in both reverse mentoring and peer mentoring, covering both the intergenerational and peer bases. Mentors should be people to whom mentees can look for guidance and inspiration. They are people who sponsor mentee development and create opportunities for them to get involved, teaching them how to be good leaders in their communities and modeling that leadership behavior.

Where we saw extraordinary intergenerational support for and mentoring of young adults, those young adults reported a willingness to "get in over their heads" in leadership positions. There was a sense that, whether they succeeded or failed, the young adults could almost do no wrong because the relationships were more important than the tasks. We also saw chosen families develop. When young adults could not easily connect with biological family members, the church family surrogated those relationships, with older members becoming "church grandmas" and "church grandpas."

Sustaining Young Adult Leadership during Transitions

Cultivating shared ownership and mentor relationships within the young adult group ensures that when there is a gap in the leadership team, another young adult can step in and make their own contributions toward nurturing a young adult group. Whether a young adult

5. Courtney L. Luedke, Dorian L. McCoy, Rachelle Winkle-Wagner, and Jamila Lee-Johnson, "Students' Perspectives on Holistic Mentoring Practices in STEM Fields," *JCSCORE* 5, no. 1 (2019): 33–59.

6. Delia S. Shelton et. al., "Expanding the Landscape of Opportunity: Professional Societies Support Early-Career Researchers through Community Programming and Peer Coaching," *Journal of Comparative Psychology* 135, no. 4 (2021): 439–49.

leader moves for a job, leaves to go be with their family, or experiences a life change such as marriage or homeownership, it places high demands on their time. Having mentor relationships established means other young adults are prepared to step into the action.

This transitional time of passing the baton from one leader to the next is called succession planning, which is key to the sustainability of any organization. Continuing the sports analogy, we can look at the handoff from one young adult leader to the next like a relay race. Lots of preparation and time has been put into preparing for the race. The young adult leader runs the first lap of the race; the person they have been mentoring and teaching watches them run the first lap and eagerly waits to receive the baton for the second lap. If something comes up in the first runner's life that requires them to exit the race, the second runner is already prepared to pick up the baton from wherever the first runner left off.

Preparation for the race is also important. Mentorship is one aspect of this, but how should the current leaders prepare the next round of leaders to run the race before the actual race day? Part of the preparation should include building up the person's belief that they could be a good leader. If they think they can be a good leader, they'll be more willing to put effort into becoming one. Young adult leaders should be connecting with those in their ministries and through those genuine connections finding out if others want to be involved in leading their groups.

Once someone has mentioned wanting to be involved in leadership, the affirmation can begin. As noted, mentoring involves providing developmental opportunities for the mentee to grow. Self-efficacy, similar to self-esteem, is important to develop within leaders. Self-efficacy is a regulatory function, meaning it allows people to exercise control over their thoughts, feelings, and actions.[7] Creating experiences that build a young adult's self-efficacy can help

7. Albert Bandura, *Social Foundations of Thought and Action: A Social Cognitive Theory* (Englewood Cliffs, NJ: Prentice-Hall, 1986).

create motivation within them to try new things, which leaders have to do. Finding times when they can get up and speak in front of their groups, coordinate events, or pray for people are some ways to help them build up confidence in themselves as leaders. If they have those opportunities, which may feel uncomfortable at first, they can look back and realize that they've done it in the past, so they can do it again. Another way to build their confidence is to have them shadow current leaders. Watching other people and learning from the way they do things is effective for aspiring leaders and their confidence levels. Creating learning moments for future leaders and having them shadow current leaders can build their leadership self-esteem and prepare them to step into the role of leaders when it is their time.

The role of church leadership in all of this is to provide support, love, and feedback. Feedback can sometimes have a negative connotation; however, the most helpful feedback is the outsider's perspective into hard situations. When young adult leaders take risks and try new things that do not go as they had hoped, getting feedback and counsel from church leaders may be helpful. Feedback should clarify uncertainty, be given soon after an event, be consistent, and come from a trusted source.[8] Treat failures as learning opportunities and provide support in those times; this will strengthen the trust between young adults and church leadership teams.

Committing through the Doldrums

Sometimes in sports, a team must rebuild from scratch after selling off "parts," or a person may change sports as they get older. What, then, do we do if the advice given above doesn't apply to a dwindling or poorly aimed ministry? In a lot of churches, this is the true test of how their cultures respond to the losses, transformations, rebirth

8. Daniel R. Ilgen, Cynthia D. Fisher, and Susan M. Taylor, "Consequences of Individual Feedback on Behavior in Organizations," *Journal of Applied Psychology* 64, no. 4 (1979): 349–71.

cycles of young adult ministries. In one sense, a ministry can, or even must, change if there is a wholesale demographic shift. This could be due to ideological issues in the group, people moving for job opportunities or better housing situations, or just normal attrition into the main congregation (what a wonderful problem that would be!). Adaptation is an important piece of DNA, in this case. Being nimble and open to new rhythms is important in leading young adult communities.

Of course, this sports analogy falls short when you consider that a church should not be a competitive space. The church ought to be able to celebrate the successful planting of a young adult in an active and supportive faith community no matter where they land, how they get there, or how briefly they stay. It is the bouncing from church to church and not finding support at any that does serious damage to young adults, taxing their spiritual lives.

The healthy church with a healthy young adult ministry ideally would elevate young adults to leadership but also be ready to bless and release them into new communities. That church also would be ready to allow its young adult ministry to go into dormancy and be able to reawaken it upon receipt of a new group of young adults ready to engage their faith.

Shared Governance and Diversity

As noted above, an important thing we learned about leadership for young adult ministries was that having a shared governance model, such as a young adult leadership team, proved to be more effective and sustainable than a model relying on a sole leader, whether that person be a pastor at the church or a young adult tasked with running the ministry. If the ministry relied on one particular person, the program could easily falter if that person became too busy or left the church for some reason. We saw several young adult ministries fold when leaders moved on to other opportunities, taking all the institutional memory with them, leaving new leaders to start from scratch.

While we do not wish to say that having a single leader never works, we have seen more success with decentralized leadership models that can weather the changes in individuals' lives, which is why we so heavily emphasize mentorship and giving multiple people opportunities to try out leadership.

When building shared governance, like a leadership team, another important factor is diversity. Young adults welcome diversity of perspective and background because they swim in this diverse pool all the time.[9] Having people of diverse lived experiences provides a space where people can genuinely learn and incorporate new worldviews into their own, thereby synthesizing stronger faith positions. Seeing diversity in leadership helps young adults feel comfortable bringing their whole selves to the group, including their faith perspective, questions, and doubts.

For example, as social justice issues arise in our country, young adults are drawn to churches that are willing to engage these issues and willing to have difficult conversations and move towards action. Often churches with diverse leadership are more prepared for these conversations and can provide young adults with the opportunities to learn from the lived experiences of the diverse people around them.

One aspect of diversity that seemed to make a difference in leadership was gender. From our observations, we noted a trend toward health and vitality when women were involved in young adult leadership. While this topic requires further study, we saw many examples of growth and the development of closer connections in young adult groups that had women in positions of leadership. In a few instances where a team's leadership changed from mostly or entirely male-led to female-led, there was almost overnight change in the attendance and enthusiasm for the group's gathering. This was true both

9. William H. Frey, "The Millennial Generation: A Demographic Bridge to America's Diverse Future," The Brookings Institution, published January 2018, http://www.brookings.edu/research/millennials.

in churches where female leadership was common and ones where male leadership was the expectation and norm.

A potential reason for this, again, is that diversity makes people more comfortable bringing their whole selves into community. Another possible reason is the sense of safety provided by having multiple genders organizing and present at group events. As noted, we have not yet formally studied gender and leadership. However, based on the stories we have heard and what we have witnessed, we do believe churches would benefit from efforts to diversify the genders involved in leadership.

In summary, churches can and should operate as resource stations for young adults in transition by recognizing young adults as leaders fully realized when they come and dwell in faithful spaces. Where some leadership models have focused on leadership as development—creating barriers and rungs on a ladder for young adults to climb prior to becoming leaders—we instead encourage churches to move toward leadership as identification by advocating for the on-ramping of young adults into leadership once they come into the community. Young adults should be involved in power sharing and reciprocal mentorship where faithful spaces adjust their expectations upward and expect more, not less, from young adults. This will in turn build commitment and trust.

Chapter Reflection Questions

1. If you have a young adult leadership team at your church, how would you characterize the relationship between that team and church leadership (pastors, elders, etc.)? What are the power dynamics like?

2. Can you think of a story that illustrates the power dynamics between the young adult leadership team and church leadership? Does this story demonstrate a good balance between providing support and allowing young adults to have autonomy?

3. Do you have any mentorship programs (official or unofficial) in place for young adults? If not, can you think of any adults in your congregation who might wish to mentor young adults?

4. If you do have mentor relationships developing, how can you include reverse mentorship practices to strengthen these relationships?

5. What is the history in your church of making decisions for and with young adults? Do you allow them to make their own decisions?

6. How have past young adult church attendees or groups of young adults been supported, or not, in their discipleship efforts? What seemed to help growth and what seemed to cause disruption or a loss of momentum?

7. What barriers, systemic or otherwise, exist to prevent young adults from participating more fully in the life of your congregation?

6

Young Adults and
New Church Models

When a Church Is Not a Church

MARTIN JIMÉNEZ

"They find us by our SEO," said the pastor of A Seattle Church. That is tech-talk for "search engine optimization," and in South Lake Union where the tech companies in Seattle congregate and headhunt one another's young, bright employees, everyone knows terms like this.

"People who are moving to Seattle or even just in town for a bit search 'diverse church' and we are one of the first hits. We literally have people show up on Sunday and that is how they described deciding to show up," says a pastor of Rainier Avenue Church in the Rainier Valley. Long considered one of America's most diverse zip codes (98118), it is hard to avoid diversity in a neighborhood that boasts fifty-nine languages.

——

As seen in our research, young adults tend to be drawn to less-established churches where they can participate more fully in building the cultural foundations of the congregations. To that end, understanding what constitutes new church developments and church plant communities can teach us what is important to serving young adults and what takes hold of their prophetic imaginations. In our work, we have studied numerous young churches, as well as long established churches, to see what the on-ramps and off-ramps for engagement are for young adults today.

Part of what moves young adults toward a feeling of belonging in a faith community is being at the start of something new that they can help build. Looking at the demographic shift in America, and around the world, reveals that new church developments have largely followed times of economic growth in the culture at large. In the early 2000s, the number of churches being planted grew at a surprising rate, and this was especially true in the Pacific Northwest. In urban areas like Seattle and Portland, church planting continues to be a method embraced by disaffected mainliners and spiritual-but-not-religious "nones" who are not ready to leave church and faith behind but prefer to move into warehouses and empty church buildings seeking something new.

In *Church Planting in Post-Christian Soil*, Chris James makes the assertion that four main typologies have presented themselves as dominant models of Seattle church planting: New Community, Household of the Spirit, Great Commission Team, and Neighborhood Incarnation. Including two more marginal categories—Sacramental Ethnic Family and Progressive Evangelical Multisites—James provides six ecclesial models that cut across different denominations and Christian subcultures to help us understand the values of those doing the church planting and, by extension, the values of the young adults who tend to be important to those expressions.[1]

---

1. Christopher B. James, *Church Planting in Post-Christian Soil* (Oxford: Oxford University Press, 2018), 232–33.

As we relate stories of the various church models where we saw young adults gravitating to around the Pacific Northwest, we'll use these broad categories to weave together both the things young adults were embracing and the challenges they faced. We aren't working exclusively with Seattle church plants in our efforts to help churches elevate young adults; however, the influence that church planting culture has in Seattle, in the region, and in the world is unmistakable. Even one-hundred-year-old churches are looking to emulate what they see in the latest church plants in Seattle coffeehouses and hand-me-down church buildings. We'll start with the most famous (or perhaps infamous) one as a way to begin discussing the Great Commission Team–style churches and Progressive Evangelical multisite churches—along with the young adult issues that they were responding to, as well as exacerbating.

The Mars Hill Story: How the Great Commission Team–Style Church Still Looms Large

Before we discuss Mars Hill Church in more detail, here is how James describes the primary ecclesial model that drives it:

> The Great Commission Team model is mission-driven ecclesiology. They understand their context as a spiritually dark and urgent mission field in need of their life-giving atonement message. Driven by desire to fulfill the task to which they have been commissioned, they strive to make disciples through missional relationships, serving, church planting, and international efforts. Their spirituality centers on obedient response to "the gospel" in both humble acknowledgement of personal sinfulness and awakening to one's missionary identity and call. The twin centers of their corporate spiritual life are missional communities—with rhythms of study, relationships, and service—and worship services that prioritize Christocentric, exegetical preaching and emotionally intense singing. Their affiliations, partnerships, and

relationships to space and context are strategically determined on the basis of their potential to advance missions. Great Commission Teams present the church as task force—a missionary team called and aided by God to make disciples.[2]

Mars Hill Church pastored by Mark Driscoll is a key example of church planting in the Great Commission Team style mixed with a bit of Evangelical Progressive multisite style, and it has shaped the theological imagination of church planting in the Pacific Northwest and beyond. This community came under fresh scrutiny in 2021 due to a *Christianity Today* podcast series by Mike Cosper. Driscoll resigned from Mars Hill in late 2014 and within months the community had dissolved. In 2016 when Pivot NW Research began its work, there was hardly a church in Seattle, including those with which we worked, that wasn't somehow affected by the fallout of the Mars Hill rise and fall. The Mars Hill story is important for our work and for the future of church plants because its mythic presence resembles what many aspire to in growing a faith community, but it also exemplifies all the cautionary realities that come when a church hurts those for whom it cares.

The following key points of the Mars Hill story are important to understanding the future of church planting, young adult faith experience, and possibly the future of the American church. Mars Hill's story is well documented and still argued over, and every other church mentioned in this chapter was doing ministry alongside, or in the wake of, that church and experienced the gravity of its ecclesiological influence on the region. In fact, some of Seattle's long-established churches, or longer-established church plants, worked with Mars Hill congregations. They may have rented space to that church in its fledgling years, or they were congregations to which the reactionary existence of Mars Hill could be partly attributed.

2. James, *Church Planting in Post-Christian Soil*, 104.

Church Plants Often Focus on the Stories and Struggles of Young Adults

Mars Hill Church tapped into young adults and intergenerational community as the dream and focus of the church. The narratives told by Mars Hill made the pain and possibilities of young adulthood prominent in ways that churches focused on either children and families or the established older generation did not. In the *Christianity Today* podcast, a former young adult who attended the church describes how this elevation of their experience drew them in:

> I think that a lot of people were good at reaching kids like me . . . people who were a little bit disenfranchised with cultural Christianity and had a little bit of that punk rock spirit, and I would say most people had some sort of heart of rebellion. That we wanted to break conventions inside and outside of church. Mars Hill embodied that spirit in many ways. The music, the aesthetics, the way they eschewed certain norms in ministry. Everything had an air of that punk rock spirit. But most of all it was embodied by Mark himself.[3]

While the view that young adults are immature and therefore not equipped to step into leadership is a commonly held conception in the American church, our research has shown that failure to give young adults roles in leadership has a negative influence on the health and welfare of a community of faith. In fact, as the data we have collected with churches over the first five years of our work shows, having young adults in leadership only deepens the faith experience of the entire church.

3. Mike Cosper, "Who Killed Mars Hill?" June 21, 2021, in *The Rise and Fall of Mars Hill*, produced by Erik Petrik, podcast, 8:00, https://www.chris tianitytoday.com/ct/podcasts/rise-and-fall-of-mars-hill/who-killed-mars -hill-church-mark-driscoll-rise-fall.html.

Church Plants Provide a Pathway for Maturity and Mentorship

As seen throughout our work, deep mentorship along with financial and spiritual resourcing are key reasons why young adults seek church communities. In an age of broken family systems and loss of confidence in authority figures and institutions, young adults still seek places of nurture and guidance to help them discover what a mature life should look like.

Generally speaking, providing pathways to maturity and leadership opportunities was a good thing and a sign of a healthy church in our observations. Cosper offers the conclusion that Mars Hill "raised young leaders where they are elevated by their ability before their character was ready."[4] This statement aligns with questions we asked throughout the course of our research: are age and character formation really that interlinked? In our experience, many young adults have shown more character and conviction germane to good leadership than their older predecessors. In the previous chapter, we enumerated ways in which young adults meet the challenge of leading in many spheres of life outside of the church but are often denied those opportunities within the church. It seemed that prior to the implosion of the Mars Hill church, many young people were asking good questions about the leadership structure and accountability of the leadership of the church.

As mentioned earlier, Mars Hill is an example of the Great Commission Team model. In fact, many of these sorts of churches in the Pacific Northwest can trace their lineage to or inspiration from the Mars Hill and Acts 29 models, even if that isn't advertised much anymore. Some are quietly carrying on the tradition of that model, having reformed its image, while others have softened the edges and sought to heal some of the wounds of that era. These defined themselves early on as hospitals for the hearts of those who sought refuge amid the fallout, but they didn't want to throw out the baby with the bathwater.

4. Cosper, "Who Killed Mars Hill?" 39:00.

Neighborhood Incarnation in a City of Neighborhoods

As young adults move to Seattle pursuing the allure of jobs in the tech industry, they may come from more conservative faith traditions elsewhere in the country and find the evangelical multisite, mega, or the Neighborhood Incarnation church plant to be an easy transitional space, given the liberal or progressive politics and culture of Seattle. In these spaces they join with like-minded mid- to long-term Seattleites who have already been living a culture of resistance against what can be seen as an overly progressive dominant culture. James describes how this can be invigorating:

> Rather than demoralizing the faithful, the minority status of confessional Christians seems to counterintuitively contribute to the vitality of their religious identity and mission. As sociologist Christian Smith has argued, Evangelicals can thrive on the sense of embattlement they feel in secularizing, pluralistic settings. The None Zone's dominant secularism has proved to be fertile environment for fervent Christianity.[5]

For these young adults, moving to urban locations like Seattle allows them freedom to restart their lives in new jobs and a new, exciting city, and it helps them form new ways of doing faith, perhaps with new opportunities for missions. In a "godless city" like Seattle, they see an opportunity to live out their faith, and their time worshipping at church equips and retools them for the evangelical struggle they live out the rest of the week at work and play. If they are planning to start a family, it is also the safe space where their faith can be practiced free of the scrutiny they would attract out in public. Often these churches, which emphasize the sort of thriving and striving that asks one to be fully committed to the *missio dei*, are located in parts of town close to where the young adults are congregating. These are full

5. James, *Church Planting in Post-Christian Soil*, 28.

of opportunities for both mission and support of the mission through jobs that can provide tithing support.

Here is how James describes Neighborhood Incarnation churches:

> Anchored in a fundamental identification with the local neighborhood as God-given parish. It is within their immediate contexts—understood as site of beauty, needs, and hope—that these followers of Jesus seek both to experience God's presence and join in God's mission. NI churches practice their neighborhood-rooted spirituality and mission through significant personal and corporate commitments to local hospitality. They seek to exist as an asset to their neighborhood, often by creating third places that facilitate meaningful relationships among members of the local community. NI churches are incarnation of Christian community in, of, and for their neighborhoods. They manifest as social bodies (Christian community) and material presences (spaces for hospitality).[6]

Multisite and network church expressions like Mars Hill were examples of the wide range of church planting visions that manifested with increasingly diverse ways for young adults to embody their unique faith approaches. Churches have names like Awake, Anchor, The Harbor, Epic Life, All Souls, Pilgrimage, Quest, Sanctuary, Restoration, Scum of the Earth, The Commons, The Garden, The Hallows, The House, Union, Vona, Wits' End. Verlon Fosner describes what these churches and the networks they formed were like in the early 2000s in his book *Dinner Church*:

> After opening up eight sites and measuring the crowd at the one-year point, we noted that (1) one-third of the attenders are financially challenged, with about half being homeless and the other half being the working poor; (2) one-third of the attenders are

6. James, *Church Planting in Post-Christian Soil*, 136.

isolated, most of whom are second-life singles—those who have already ruined one life and are desperately hoping not to ruin another; and (3) the good Samaritans who live in the neighborhood, most of whom are millennials, joining the Christians to befriend, serve, and lift everyone else in the room. That has become the milieu of our dinner churches.[7]

Both Mars Hill Church and Dinner Church, along with any of the other dozens of new faith communities in Seattle, in their diverse ways give the large population of young adults a sense of "identity, belonging, and purpose," which are themes that the Fuller Youth Institute has named as the three primary virtues that young adults seek in communities of faith. As outlined in previous chapters and made clear from dozens of examples in churches and church plants in Seattle, a church or church plant must offer opportunities for young adults to actively germinate, take root, and grow, not just observe others practice faith from the sidelines. Churches that assume young adults can't commit or want an easy, simple faith are selling short everyone who is involved. Even as attractive as Mars Hill Church was at its height, being a multisite church attempting to incarnate in multiple neighborhoods of Seattle is difficult when the average young adult is entering adulthood without savings, high salary potential, or traditional safety nets intact. In *Dinner Church,* Verlon Fosner writes about the realization that many of the core families of the church had long since moved away from the neighborhood for any number of reasons (bigger houses or more land for a growing family, employment, proximity to family, weariness of city hubbub, and so on).[8] This meant the community needed to relearn a theology of neighborhood and hospitality as both guest and host. It also needed to be reoriented around what it means to live in the city as a young

7. Verlon Fosner, *Dinner Church: Building Bridges by Breaking Bread* (Franklin, TN: Seedbed Publishing, 2017), 31.
8. Fosner, *Dinner Church,* 107.

adult with fewer resources and smaller spaces, and to live among other working or retired poor. For older adults already in Seattle as homeowners, living incarnationally in their neighborhood context might come more naturally. In the conclusion, we will look closer at the effects of financial poverty interrelated with the realities of young adult faith and other areas of poverty (mental health, physical health, relationship health, etc.).

When young adults do make sacrifices to live in their chosen neighborhood where they want to worship and live, it often means living in much smaller spaces because of affordability. In the last decade, the size of newly built apartments in Seattle has dropped from just under 900 square feet to just over 635 square feet.[9] This then leads to further dynamics regarding perceptions of power and bandwidth because young adults in positions of more stress and fewer resources can often be expected to participate in equal amount to those who have enjoyed home equity growth, continued employment, and less overall disruption in their life.

One important reason for growth in multisite churches is because of affordability issues for young adults and their young families. Carol Merritt in *The Tribal Church* puts it this way: "The economic situation affects everything in a young adult's life, and it has a huge impact on their ability to form committed relationships. Many people in their twenties and thirties often find that they cannot bind themselves to loving relationships, civic institutions, or spiritual communities because they cannot make the commitment of finances, time, or trust."[10] Churches in urban contexts feel a double pull to make suburban church plants: from young families in search of affordability and family-friendly neighborhoods on the one hand, and from Boomer

9. Sarah Anne Lloyd, "New Seattle Apartments Have Shrunk Almost 30% in 15 Years," Curbed Seattle, November 2, 2017, https://seattle.curbed.com /2017/11/2/16599858/seattle-apartment-size-shrinking-data.

10. Carol H. Merritt, *The Tribal Church: Ministering to the Missing Generation* (Herndon, VA: The Alban Institute, 2007), 138.

funding on the other. Bethany Community Church is a good example of the multisite model. The church plants, or in this case multisite churches, incarnate their neighborhood, city, or regional ministry identity and intermix whatever culture they bring with them with whatever culture they land in.

Relocation, Replanting, and the Challenge of Language: Are You a Colonizer, Gentrifier, or Incarnator?

Have any churches planted in Seattle left their location altogether because of cost or opportunity? Yes, this has been the story of several churches in the region, and one of our research churches, Renew Church in Lynnwood, provides an example. Originally a North Seattle church plant with the Evangelical Covenant Church denomination, Renew Church had an opportunity to redefine its mission in an entirely different city in the northern suburbs of Seattle. The bulk of its members moved their worship home north from a community center into a denomination-owned church building where they immediately became landlords for a handful of other ethnic-based worshipping communities and stewards of a property that was located near a community transportation hub. The cheaper cost of living changed their demographic and ministry strategy almost overnight as they struggled to weather the change in incarnation. They also took on a symbiotic relationship with the congregations they host, which might fit James's Household of the Spirit and Sacramental Ethnic Family models.

In many ways, the young adults on Renew's leadership team felt unprepared to be thrust into a parental or caretaking role for the other congregations sharing their new worship space. Working on innovative church models within existing church structures comes naturally to young adults who are used to the church telling them they need to wait in the wings until they are proven, matured, or ready to take on responsibilities. But this insistence on a tempering period falls away when a desperate denomination has space but no people and finds itself looking for occupants.

The irony of Renew's movement from North Seattle to Lynnwood is that it had been in conversation with that exact congregation about merging ministries a few years earlier, but there were too many cultural differences for Renew to seriously consider the merger at that time. In a Jonah-like moment, it was later approached by the denomination as a healthy, young, vital community that could use a more permanent home and ministry space. This story offers a clear picture of how a church that is led by young adults and puts them front and center can find itself with options for thriving.

With these relocations where a church is planting, moving, or otherwise serving in a non-native space, questions of colonialism and power dynamics arise from both young and older adults. Renew and other churches we have worked with have had to do some soul-searching regarding both the legacies they received and the legacies they are being asked to build. The colonialization of the city's poorer neighborhoods is often discussed by another name: gentrification.

Is gentrification a necessary cost of doing business as a Neighborhood Incarnational church? This is the sort of question that is actively on the minds of churches in Seattle, especially among young adult Christians. The gentrification of neighborhoods in Seattle is and has been affecting both church plants and established churches for several years now, creating new challenges when these churches try to connect with neighbors. One might ask whether the gentrification of neighborhoods is aided and abetted by the church, but in a city as unchurched as Seattle, that is probably giving the churches too much credit. There are few, if any, churches that have the money and cultural power to effect the same sort of change that comes easy to developers, landlords, and other moneyed interests raising rents and redeveloping neighborhoods such that they become unaffordable to the historic tenants.

The active gentrification that was clearest among Pivot NW Research church partners was probably in the Rainier Valley at Rainier Avenue Church, a Free Methodist congregation whose young adults had a front seat to the change. How does a church incarnate in a neighborhood that is changing so drastically? The Rainier Valley neighborhood has eighteen non-English languages primarily spoken at home, and the community is 80 percent nonwhite.[11] But an influx of young tech workers who come from diverse backgrounds and are looking for cheap housing, along with transit improvements and the reversal of suburban flight, have caused tensions between the new residents and the old core communities of color. Outrage at the influx of wealth and cries of "the Valley is for poor people" were heard loudly in 2006 when transit expansion was announced at a community meeting.[12] In this neighborhood, churches of poorer immigrant communities could survive under the radar—churches that fall into the cross section that James might codify as Sacramental Ethnic Family and Household of the Spirit that brought practices and cultures from other continents. In some ways, Rainier Valley looks a lot like the global Christianity found in other Western countries that have seen an influx of migrants fleeing war and famine. And caught in the crossfire between historic residential ethnic groups and private and public redevelopment interests are young adults trying to survive, if not thrive, in their emergent adulthood.

Leroy Barber writes that "in missions, we share the Gospel and, implicitly, our culture. But when we insist others give up *their* culture for Christianity, we become colonizers. *Missio Dei* is not a call to culturalize and patronize nonbelievers; rather, it is a delivering the Gospel without judgment or cultural bias. A decision to devote your life to mission means you agree to represent the heart of God as best you can and as accurately as you can."[13] While Barber is writing

11. City of Seattle, "Rainier Beach Neighborhood Snapshot," Seattle Department of Neighborhoods, published August 2019, http://www.seattle.gov/Documents/Departments/Neighborhoods/Districts/Neighborhood%20Snapshots/Rainier-Beach-Snapshot.pdf.

12. David Leong, *Race and Place: How Urban Geography Shapes the Journey to Reconciliation* (Downers Grove, Il: IVP Books, 2017), 129–30.

13. Leroy Barber, *Red, Brown, Yellow, Black, White—Who's More Precious in God's Sight? A Call for Diversity in Christian Missions and Ministry* (New York: Jericho Books, 2014), 4.

specifically about white dominance of urban, intercultural spaces, his words ring true for white dominance of international neighborhoods where immigrants find refuge in affordable communities near growing urban metropolises—communities such as Rainier Valley.

Young adults know that joining a church often means giving up parts of their own culture and adopting that of the church. So, in a way, not only is colonization physically happening in our communities by white-dominant churches following missional calls to inhabit neighborhoods for the purpose of spreading the gospel, but also as a microcosm in the lives of young adults negotiating their faith life. In his 1996 book *Exclusion and Embrace*, Miroslav Volf describes this as exclusion by assimilation, wherein people are only accepted into a community after they have been exorcised of characteristics foreign to the community.[14] This becomes an obstacle and a trade-off that many young adults can't stomach because to them it means giving up leisure time and time with peers to engage in difficult interactions with cultural strangers who have high expectations that they adopt forms of Christianity that are bound to past cultural and societal norms. The energy likely would seem to them to be more wisely spent building the next, evolved instance of the church rather than giving life support to the current, dying version, and it is hard to debate that logic.

Do you prioritize the assimilation of young adults into the culture of the church? Or would you be willing to allow a young adult who seems somewhat wild and untamed to move the church's vision more toward a hermeneutic that doesn't always fit the church's established orthodoxy? Again, we learn from Barber that the assimilation process threatens whatever native passion and insight an identified leader might bring into an organization that will help it be effective and organically evolve.[15]

---

14. Miroslav Volf, *Exclusion and Embrace: A Theological Exploration of Identity, Otherness, and Reconciliation* (Nashville: Abingdon, 1996), 75.

15. Barber, *Red, Brown, Yellow, Black, White*, 8.

Under a subheading titled "Culture Eats Strategy for Breakfast," which repurposes Peter Drucker's famous phrase, Tim Soerens suggests that "to build local culture and embody an alternative story, we need a team." He continues, "Neither evangelism nor discipleship makes much sense unless we can craft a public way of life together that becomes a plausibility structure that claims the gospel is true."[16] Soerens's conclusion is that *relationship* within a team is key to creating a beneficial culture that is mutually supportive and synergistic. We can affirm this by our own observations of the young adult leadership teams formed at our participating churches. When young adults and older adults form relationships in the context of a committed team (in this case an intergenerational one at times), a new or renewed culture arises on the basis of empathy, trust, and healthy differentiation. They all bring in separate stories, but at some point they share a story that informs a commonly held culture. It is a synthesis, a synergy.

Another concept that is in vogue to describe this strategy is that of a "guiding coalition" whereupon over time a transformation effort can be led by a critical mass of stakeholders.[17] Additionally, as those stakeholders spend time working together on the same project, they engage in mutual transformation as their intimacy creates positive empathy—even if the project is a failure or the experience is negative.

As previously mentioned, Rainier Avenue Church is an expression of the Free Methodist denomination and is therefore situated within the holiness tradition, which holds to many theologically and culturally traditional and conservative views. That said, the young adults we worked with in the congregation are quite progressive on several issues. As a team built on trust and relationships, the young adults at Rainier Avenue Church do not seek to antagonize the more

16. Tim Soerens, *Everywhere You Look: Discovering the Church Right Where You Are* (Downers Grove, IL: Intervarsity Press, 2020), 72.

17. John P. Kotter, "Leading Change: Why Transformation Efforts Fail," *Harvard Business Review* 73, no. 2 (1995): 59–67.

traditional leadership in their church but respect their legacy and continued commitment to the faith. As they work and live in a more diverse reality, however, they serve their community with a progressive fervor through a microgrant program that they established to better help build their diverse community as an expression of their faith. Service to the community is a core theme for all members of the congregation, but the young adults have found a way to express their more progressive, expansive commitments that makes a direct impact on the community through these microgrants while also holding firm to their community and legacy as a Free Methodist congregation.

New Community-Style Churches

Still another ecclesial model is that of New Community, which James describes in this way:

> Churches in the New Community model embody a practical ecclesiology that is at once eschatological in its underlying vision and institutional in its concrete identity. In stark contrast to the Evangelicals whose countercultural postures have left many participants disillusioned, NC churches celebrate the social progressivism of their context as a foreshadowing of the new humanity they seek to embody in their authentic fellowship. Their community embodiment of inclusive and participatory corporate life is their chief form of witness. At the center of their practice is worship that integrates ancient and institutional liturgical practices with contemporary arts and technology, thus exercising their identity as mainline innovators. The open Communion table at the center of their worship enacts the gospel of God's unqualified welcome into community and reflects their embrace of the mysterious and ambiguous presence of God hidden in everyday embodied life.[18]

18. James, *Church Planting in Post-Christian Soil*, 125.

David Leong, a professor and member of Rainier Avenue Church, spells out the difficulty of reconciliation once we have an awareness of otherwise erased populations such as the indigenous Duwamish peoples who are some of Seattle's original inhabitants.[19] It is perhaps no wonder that when Leong searches in his neighborhood for a church that is trying to embody a nongentrifying presence, he looks to a young church planter, John Helmiere, and the Hillman City Collaboratory. Leong describes it as a place where the values are "listening, hospitality, and liberation for the common good of the neighborhood." Leong continues, "John (Helmiere) has simply cultivated friendships across traditional boundaries and joined in true partnerships with the good folks who are making ends meet and looking for a place to call their own. Together, they are dreaming about the possibilities of what is birthed in our shared gardening, cooking, music making, and laughter around the table."[20] Young adults generally seem to want their church's theological and cultural expression to be in sync with that of their neighbors, not at odds. But sometimes that means being at odds with the internal dominant culture of their congregation, a situation not unlike the cultural assimilation issues of the Pauline epistles. While Paul gave a lot of specific advice to the Corinthian church, the overwhelming message was to marginalize thoughts and behaviors that separated the church's members from God, which included both gross immorality in business and relationships, but also pharisaical behavior.

Perhaps this is most important in the New Community type church that James identifies as an expression of faith that embodies progressive and inclusive values that bring to the fore collective social justice action, denominational partnership, and worship service and community involvement. While most churches don't fit into this model (according to James about 10 percent of his sample of 112 church plants),[21] it has become an important reference for the future of the church, given the lifetime of relationship with more and more diverse

---

19. Leong, *Race and Place*.
20. Leong, *Race and Place*, 152–53.
21. James, *Church Planting in Post-Christian Soil*, 112.

communities that Generation X and subsequent generations have had. Diversity exists not just in the form of ethnic background and other cultural markers that churches are used to navigating, but also in unfamiliar forms such as sexual preference and gender identity. While the prominence of young adults in the New Community is beyond the scope of James's work, many of the young adults we work with in our study are seen as prophets and leaders more easily because of the investment in exorcising preconceived notions of ability and calling. That isn't to say that the New Community church style is perfect or preferred, as none of the models that James presents integrates the issues important to young adults perfectly in our estimation. But a core value to most young adults is the validation of their communities, which are the most diverse ones yet in America. And they become more diverse with each generation. Young adults have flatly told us they do not want to lead, or even participate in, churches that reject their friends, colleagues, and family members as unrepentant sinners based on things like sexual attraction, gender identity, and other divisive issues of the last few decades. Not only does this rub against the stereotype that young adults are "self-centered," but it shows how radically other- or group-centered they are.

Household of the Spirit

The smallest subsection of churches we encountered with young adult participants was the Household of the Spirit type. James describes them like this:

> Households of the Spirit gather to experience the presence of a miracle-working God in a foreign and fallen land. Their spirituality centers on emotionally charged worship events that proclaim and produce experiences of God's sensible immanence and miracle-working power. They stress the need to live obedient lives of biblical faith in holiness, devotion, public witness, and financial giving. While they seek to foster an environment and community safe and set apart, they also actively invite others into

the sanctuary community, and stress going out to offer supernatural blessings and healing prayers to others. This practical ecclesiological model presents the church as a temple of God's powerful presence and an extended family of faith called and empowered by the Spirit to offer supernatural healing in a sin-sick world.[22]

Like churches in the Sacramental Ethnic Family, these types of churches and church plants are more likely to be suspicious of an effort like Pivot NW Research and are more likely to trust in-house teaching and formation that has familiar language and structure. In that way, we observe they are also more likely to be naturally intergenerational. Given that the Pentecostal, charismatic, and other traditions that primarily make up this grouping are parts of a relatively young tradition (one hundred to two hundred years old), there has been less time for stagnation of practice to create exclusionary hierarchies based on age. Because the training and ordination process is less formal in these traditions, young adult leaders tend to be recruited early and personally trained by mentors in repeated patterns that help them to be more intergenerational. Yet some of the same issues of recruiting nonordained young adults in church councils and having a diverse group of young adults interacting with a homogenous group of older adults are just as present as in every other group. They arise in the same way as in other church expressions, since the same sociological conditions of older-generation control and younger-generation suspicion exist across American and Pacific Northwest social constructs.

Young adults in most any type of church will eventually face a decision of whether to commit to the church long term, follow a call to a different community, or maybe just sit in limbo until the decision becomes clear. This choice may present itself more than once, and we would be remiss not to point out that it is an ongoing issue in adulthood as one reaches ages and stages that cause a shuffling of values. In young adulthood, however, there can be a lack of clarity or an anxiety that comes with that.

22. James, *Church Planting in Post-Christian Soil*, 112.

One example of a young adult group having to decide its own fate in relation to the larger congregation is that of Lighthouse Community Church. Lighthouse doesn't fall neatly into any of the categories James suggests, but it does have a strong culture of internal leadership promotion and intergenerational community. Lighthouse is a largely pan-Asian American congregation that gathers east of Seattle near Microsoft's headquarters. It has a community consciousness where newcomers would come into the group from outside the church community and, at some point, decide to either join the intergenerational core of the congregation or pursue a different direction as a group or individually.

The current young adults who are all young millennials are having to negotiate a history marked by a Generation X group of young adults who together made a mass induction into the core of the congregation, which is no doubt part of the church's current manifestation of strength and sustainability. Various options on the table were for the group to (1) slowly splinter into the mainstream of that church and others, (2) plant their own church as a group of young adults wanting to forge their own way forward, or (3) try to create a different model that wouldn't decimate the young adult ministry every few years with a mass graduation but rather would try to manage the tension of new young adults continually coming in and older young adults continually transitioning into the core congregational body. It is to the credit of everyone involved (Lighthouse pastors and congregation, young adults and their leaders, and those straddling all of those identities) that there were several solutions to the future faith of the young adults that all seemed viable and beneficial to both the larger group and the individual constituents. So, how do churches of any stripe survive these eventual questions of transition?

Young Adult Program Transitions:
Succession, Sustainability, and Incidental Church Planting

In prior chapters, we have discussed the personal transitions of young adults and the contexts they are moving into and out of, both in the church and in the secular realms they occupy. But how does the church transition to meet the presence and absence of young adults?

This is a reality for University Presbyterian Church (UPC), a large mainline congregation near the University of Washington in Seattle that has a long history of working closely with university students and faculty, and that increasingly found that their young adult ministry overlapped considerably with their international ministry. There were many twentysomethings from other countries who were looking for already-built Christian community to join while they were temporarily in country. In a way, UPC was in the difficult position to either provide community to international students with the understanding that it could be a revolving door, or instead focus on providing community for another group of young adults who may be more permanent but just aren't searching for community. Time and time again, we heard from both young and older adults that working in the international ministry at UPC gave them a sense of purpose and faithfulness that grounded their faith as much or more than other ministry opportunities at the church. Involvement with this intergenerational ministry is an important factor for young adults as they consider whether to stay at UPC as they age or stage out of young adulthood, showing the value of relationship building beyond a young adult-focused program.

The young adult ministries at UPC, Lake Burien Presbyterian Church, and Lighthouse each worked to have the larger congregation move closer toward the young adult ministry, so that instead of being at the siloed edge, the ministry became central to its body and, perhaps, even overlapped with other core missions and leadership. This is essentially a redefinition or realignment of the church's holistic ministry with the missional opportunities knocking at its door.

A clear example of a church whose young adult-centered expression is an actual plant is that of Northminster Presbyterian Church and its relationship with Coastland Commons. Part of a 2012 Presbyterian Church USA initiative named 1001 New Worshipping Communities, Coastland Commons is a nested worshipping community that relies on the support of the centennial-aged Northminster Presbyterian Church and even partners in some ministries, shared staff, and buildings, but it has a separate governing body and little crossover with the membership of the host church. In this case, the relationship is two-way with the ministry priorities and activities of Coastland Commons spilling over into Northminster and informing the practice of the host church. Justice, inclusion, engagement of fine and performing arts, and reflection and spiritual growth are all emphases that find new vitality at Coastland Commons, to the delight of the host congregation. There are points of collaboration in acts of music, food, and a joint ministry of letter-writing to incarcerated women.

Bottom Line: Help Young Adults Find Safety, Security, and Belonging

Young adulthood, much like young churchhood (i.e., church planting), is full of unknowns, insecurity, and transience. But familial relationships, both intergenerational and among peers, can help ground someone when most other factors are failing. While some of the young adults in our study are grounded in marriages, careers, or even parenthood, the lion's share of them are struggling to find stable and affordable housing, careers that they can count on for wealth and a sense of vocational calling, reasons to eke it out in Seattle rather than move back home, and so on. In the exploration of this concept, many young adults in progressive, urban centers like Seattle are leaning in to the LGBTQIA+ community and finding models of care and hope. Because many have been rejected by families who cannot fathom their queerness, they crave the radical acceptance of communities that invite them into a secure, familial relationship. In some of our churches, that is expressly integrated into the expression of the community (think rainbow flags and "all are welcome" signs). In others, the expression is born out of a desire to live faithfully to Scripture and is more muted. Either way, the Pacific Northwest is still a place where people arrive after feeling called to leave their families and old ways behind, striking out west to redefine themselves and find communities in which they can become more fully themselves.

The bottom line is that if a church can give young adults a sense of familial belonging and support, whether it is the international graduate student at UPC, the fresh-faced Amazon employee at A Seattle Church, the young adult exploring their sense of gender identity within the safe space of Coastland Commons, or someone living in the tension of a traditional and progressive community like Rainier Avenue Church, young adults will consider the church a fertile place to grow a taproot of love and acceptance, even if sooner or later they are called elsewhere.

Chapter Reflection Questions

1. What is your experience with church planting, church death, or moving from one church to the next? What was the set of circumstances, whether beneficial or toxic, that surrounded those experiences and transition questions?
2. What would you consider your "found" or "chosen" family? How does that theology fit into your life, and how does it challenge you?
3. When have you encountered an atypical leader in the church and how did that challenge you?
4. When did you create a relationship in the church through a failed effort or maybe just an unrecognized struggle? When did you create relationship through a successful effort or leadership challenge? What has that taught you about the reward of coworking or working across generational divides?
5. What would you say is a prophetic edge or challenge for your church?
6. When did your church stop being considered a church plant? What stories surrounding that suggest any privilege or lack of privilege of the time, place, and constitution of those planting the church?

Conclusion

Active Love and the Hope of Communities of Loving Defiance

JEFFREY F. KEUSS

> I am not scared of death, I've got dreams again
> It's just me and the curve of the valley
> And there is meanin' on earth, I am happy . . .
> I'm back between villages and everything's still.
>
> —Noah Kahan, "The View between Villages"

In the study of new ecclesiologies and how young adults find on-ramps and off-ramps into and out of faith communities,[1] it doesn't take long for the question of responsive and emancipatory economics to enter the conversation as one of the primary ways that Christians should be engaging contemporary culture.

For example a Pew Research Center study showed that

an estimated 5.3 million of the nearly seventeen million United States households living in poverty were headed by a millennial, compared with 4.2 million headed by a Gen Xer and five million headed by a baby boomer. The relatively high number of millen-

1. Pivot NW Research, https://pivotnw.org/about/.

nial households in poverty partly reflects the fact that the poverty rate among households headed by a young adult has been rising over the past half century while dramatically declining among households headed by those sixty-five and older. In addition, millennials are more racially and ethnically diverse than the other adult generations and a greater share of millennial households are headed by minorities, who tend to have higher poverty rates. Millennial heads of households are also more likely to be unmarried, which is associated with higher poverty.[2]

According to another Pew study,

compared with earlier generations, more millennials have outstanding student debt, and the amount of it they owe tends to be greater. The share of young adult households with student debt doubled from 1998 (when Gen Xers were ages twenty to thirty-five) to 2016 (when millennials were that age). In addition, the median amount of debt was nearly 50 percent greater for millennials with outstanding student debt ($19,000) than for Gen X debt holders when they were young ($12,800).[3]

The growing sense of losing ground in the marketplace, both in slower gains in income coupled with greater debt, is coupled with a deeper poverty: a poverty of hope and agency that is seen not only in lack of capital but in spiritual and emotional despair and anxiety. Where financial metrics for the aftershocks of late capitalism and the labor opportunities of the free market are plentiful, they tell only

2. Richard Fry, "Five Facts about Millennial Households," Pew Research Center, September 6, 2017, https://www.pewresearch.org/fact-tank/2017/09/06/5-facts-about-millennial-households/.

3. "Millennial Life: How Young Adulthood Compares Today with Prior Generations," Pew Research Center, February 14, 2019, https://www.pewresearch.org/social-trends/2019/02/14/millennial-life-how-young-adulthood-today-compares-with-prior-generations-2/.

part of the story, and the effects are seen in the younger generations. The Centers for Disease Control and Prevention (CDC) reports that one in five American children ages three through seventeen—about 15 million—have a diagnosable mental, emotional, or behavioral disorder in a given year. Only 20 percent of these children are ever diagnosed and receive treatment; 80 percent—about 12 million—aren't receiving treatment. Recent research indicates that serious depression is worsening in teens, especially girls, and the suicide rate among girls reached a forty-year high in 2015, according to a CDC report released in August.[4] In our research through Pivot NW Research,[5] the disconnect and lack of bridging between economic concerns and spiritual and psychological malaise is one reason young adults view the church as irrelevant. In order to better on-ramp young adults to communities that can provide the integration of body, soul, and spirit, it is imperative to speak not only to material poverty but also to the larger reality of deep poverty in our time.

Deep Poverty: Healing Body, Soul, and Spirit

At stake in what I am terming "deep poverty" is the holistic concern of the whole person located in systems where access to the market must be related to access to communities of spiritual and psychological nurture. Traditional metrics of wealth and poverty have been found wanting in helping to comprehend the deep poverty evident in young adults, and the current upheaval in relation to the ever-growing rift between the "haves" and the "have nots" is not slowing either in material or spiritual health. Deep poverty is poverty that is not measured solely by conventional economic indicators such as gross

4. "Mental Health Conditions: Anxiety and Depression," Centers for Disease Control and Prevention, accessed September 14, 2022, https://www.cdc.gov/tobacco/campaign/tips/diseases/depression-anxiety.html.
5. Pivot NW, "Young Adults and the Church in the Pacific Northwest and U.S.: 2017–2018 Study," Retrieved on November 23, 2019: https://pivotnw.org/research.

national product or cost of living indexes, but a deeper understanding of poverty *qua* poverty where financial uncertainty is a symptom of a deeper spiritual and psychic crisis in our time that includes loss of hope, lack of support, and gross marginality of people groups.

As a theologian, I see this pointing to the church's call to witness. How do we (as the body of Christ) embody a responsive economic witness in the world that moves beyond rhetoric and into praxis that reflects the call of Philippians 2—emptying ourselves and taking the form of servants? How do we as the church acknowledge the deep poverty of the whole person and not merely either the lack of capital or the lack of spiritual vitality as separate concerns?

My hope in the remainder of this chapter is to address these questions by outlining some of the opportunities brought forth from the twilight of modernism and the dawn of postmodern critique as well as the resources from a centrist reading of Scripture toward some application of Ron Sider's work engaging spiritual and economics disciplines that young adults—alongside all members of the church—can practice in the face of deep poverty.

Active Love and Deep Poverty in the Soil of Postmodernism

As Carl Raschke has pointed out in his book *The Next Reformation*, postmodernity has raised, not lowered, the bar for the body of Christ as to what humble form our collective lives should take for the sake of the call of Jesus Christ.[6] This call to humility is not merely a spiritual exercise but a Leviticus 25 holistic call of Jubilee and Sabbath. Over and over in our research with young adults in the Pacific Northwest, we continue to hear that they deeply desire evidence of real humility in the face of the embodied, difficult issues in our culture. This is key to connecting young people to communities of faith.

In some respects, this is what Dostoevsky in *The Brothers Kara-mazov* challenged his contemporaries in the nineteenth century to

6. Carl Raschke, *The Next Reformation: Why Evangelicals Must Embrace Postmodernity* (Grand Rapids: Baker Academic, 2004).

CONCLUSION

embrace as active love: "Try to love your neighbors actively and tirelessly. The more you succeed in loving, the more you'll be convinced of the existence of God and the immortality of your soul. And if you reach complete selflessness in the love of your neighbor, then undoubtedly you will believe."[7] What Dostoevsky termed "active love" in the nineteenth century is in concert with the embodied activism and responses to deep poverty seen and heard in the lives of young adults today. Part of what forms this desire to respond to deep poverty through active love is seen in the philosophical and theological soil within which many young adults have been formed today: postmodernism.

Some have been dismissive of the role postmodern critique can have in assisting with solving the current and urgent questions of our time. As Tyron Inbody notes, some too readily dismiss the postmodern critique of late capitalism as merely "intellectual Velcro dragged across culture" that "can be used to characterize almost anything one approves or disapproves."[8] Or, as Umberto Eco quipped, postmodernism "is applied today to anything the users of the term happen to like."[9] In Raschke's estimation, American evangelicalism has at times been reticent to utilize the tools of postmodern critique to reengage the gospel in our cultural context and, in the end, it has only reinforced systems of economic slavery in the name of gospel.

Rather than dismissing the critique too readily, this paradigm shift in Western philosophical tradition called "postmodernism" has perhaps made ready our culture for encountering the challenge of deep poverty. Daniel Adams made this point clear: "It is obvious that modernism as an ideology of Western culture is in serious trouble. At the present time, however, no one knows for certain what will arise to take modernism's place. The postmodern is the name given

7. Fyodor Dostoevsky, *The Brothers Karamazov*, trans. Richard Pevear and Larissa Volokhonsky (New York: Farrar, Straus & Giroux, 1880, 1990), 56.
8. Tyron Inbody, "Postmodernism: Intellectual Velcro Dragged across Culture," *Theology Today* 57, no. 4 (January 1995): 524.
9. Umberto Eco, *Postscript to The Name of the Rose*, trans. William Weaver (San Diego: Harcourt Brace Jovanovich, 1989), 65.

to this space between what was and what is yet to be."[10] As we attempt to frame the global aspects of a new measure for deep poverty and grounded economic reflection, it is helpful to review some of the characteristics and themes that are prevalent in our current cultural moment.

Four Characteristics of Postmodernism in Relation to Deep Poverty[11]

When considering the systems that contribute to the deep poverty in our culture as the lived experience of young adults, four key indicators can be seen both culturally and theologically as movements since the nineteenth century. The first indicator is what is seen as the decline of the West as a figure of reference for what constitutes what is "normative" in economic indicators. With the birth of multinational globalism after the fall of the Berlin Wall, the rise of China as a serious player in the free market, the history of World Trade Organization protests, the recent uprisings in Hong Kong, and the idealistic hope that birthed the European Union as a real economic entity that provides a hybrid for former Eastern bloc countries with Western economic philosophical thought, the world has become much larger and much smaller at the same time. While the force of the United States in the world market remains a dominant (at times domineering) reality, the number of viable decision markets has increased not merely in name but in deed. In short, cultural and national boundaries are eroding to the point of becoming merely public relations theory. New global strategic alliances continue to evolve and challenge the West as a primary force.

10. Daniel J. Adams, "Toward a Theological Understanding of Postmodernism," *Cross Currents* 47, no. 4 (Winter 1997–1998).

11. Zygmunt Bauman, *Intimations of Postmodernity* (London: Routledge, 1992), 35–52, 96–101; John W. Cooper, "Reformed Apologetics and the Challenge of Post-modern Relativism," *Calvin Theological Journal* 28, no. 1 (April 1993): 109–10.

Second, the loss of the West as a prime and solitary force in the twentieth century has resulted in the legitimization or authority crisis: the challenge faced in the midst of the postmodern turn has been in finding a foundational authoritative voice or voices from which to reconcile contrary or differing views. In regard to the economic questions related to deep poverty, rather than being a threat to stable economic indicators, this proves both a challenge and an opportunity to allow other voices to enter into the dialogue and the democracy of voices to arise where authority is not merely invested through having the largest gross national product. When Jesus asked the question "Who do you say that I am?" (Matt. 16:15), he was raising the question of authority.

With this anxiety surrounding authority figures, we see the third movement which in the twentieth century is the rise of the intellectual marketplace. Karl Marx moved the critique of capitalism forward with his statement that one needs only look to the means of production to understand where true economic power lies. As the world has moved out of the industrial age of the Victorian period and into the twenty-first century, the value of "intellectual property" (IP) has transformed the marketplace and tipped the economics of the world to where, as seen with the rise of the dot-com era in the late 1990s on through today, the value of ideas over products in the twenty-first century has fully dawned. This is potentially an incredible opportunity for the world where the go-to-market speed has increased, and the ability to bring ideas to investors continues to be a viable trade option.

Lastly, moving out of the twentieth century and into the twenty-first century, we have seen the effects of the process of deconstruction and the hunger for connectedness through diversity as a drive for young adults. As discussed by Shin Kuk-Won, professor of philosophy at Chongshin University in Seoul, South Korea, in his article "Postmodernism and a Christian Response," the centrist view of the world is one where the dominant locus of thought has evaporated under the rejection of Enlightenment presuppositions of classical metaphysical thought.[12] What has risen is the voice of the individual always preceding the communal. In addition, with the loss of the communal sense of identity, the individual is left with personal reason or emotion as the primary means of testing truth claims. Yet there is also a hunger for connectedness—a desire to be tethered to others in affinity groups, as opposed to alliances born of citizenship or membership. This is one of the great challenges as the need to build a new vision for citizenship and civic responsibility continues to be questioned by a younger generation shaped by deep suspicion of institutions and governments that seem to ask the individual to submit agency to the collective either implicitly or explicitly. While the term "deconstruction" may send a chill up the spine of some people of faith, it is certainly providing a renewed opportunity to ask how this shift to philosophically and theologically reject the assumption of human autonomy in favor of connectedness can be bridged into a vision for citizenship in the twenty-first century.

Five Assumptions on God's Call and Response to Holistic Life in the Midst of Deep Poverty

This shift away from a Western economic and philosophical dominance, the move toward a more diffused global economic platform, the suspicion toward member-seeking institutions as opposed to connectedness that highlights the individual as an embodied person with a diverse understanding of self—all these things provide the church with exciting opportunities to address and move into. As we have seen throughout our work, young adults are still seeking a path to answer the questions of deep poverty for themselves and others. They want a life worth living alongside others. Scripture offers some important guidelines that provide vectors for establishing a means for engagement and a measuring

---

12. This is briefly outlined in Shin Kuk-Won, "Postmodernism and a Christian Response," *Pro Rege* 22, no. 4 (June 1994): 15–25, especially 17–18, http://www.dordt.edu/publications/pro_rege/crcpi/95097.pdf.

line for what God values in relation to our economic and spiritual view of the world that resonates with the cultural form that postmodernism offers. Here are five assumptions drawn from Scripture:

1. *God owns all things.* As we hear in Psalm 24:11 and Job 41:11, the notion of personal and corporate ownership is an illusion. We have a *lease relationship* with this life. The fact that people speak of "owning" a home when the truth of the matter is that a vast majority of so-called homeowners are more or less like tenants in residences that can be taken away by mortgage companies or banks shows how far we have come as a culture into the illusion that debt can be equated with true ownership. This mentality has seeped into the marrow of our understanding of God's ownership of creation and all that dwells in it. Regardless of one's stance on free will and human ethical agency, it is central to the Christian story that God is not only the sustainer of creation, but the owner as well. We are stewards of the garden, not owners. Yet the danger of seeking dominance and mastery is always before us. As John Taylor points out in his book *Enough Is Enough*:

> Only in the unbroken awareness of God is humanity's technological mastery safe. Only in the acceptance of creaturehood can humanity's dominion over creation be prevented from becoming raw domination. Being answerable to God humanity remains answerable for their fellow creature and for the soil of the earth.[13]

2. *God provides all things.* As Scripture reminds us, there is no need for anxiety (Matt. 6; Luke 12:22–31); no need for love of money (Heb. 13:5); no need to serve two masters (Matt. 6:24); no need to seek secondary treasures (Matt. 13:45). In short, what is needed is provided for—all the rest is fuel for fear, at best. Part of the concerns surrounding economic flux in the global market and the rash responses— from Y2K paranoia at the end of the twentieth century to increased interest in Middle East oil reserves—has to do with a need to manage

---

13. John Vernon Taylor, *Enough Is Enough* (London: SCM, 1975), 53.

and control those things we need due to our deep lack of faith. In short, we merely pay lip service to God's providence when we hoard goods and services unto ourselves at the expense of others. The notion that we are to focus on our own people per se as the prime directive only exacerbates the divide between our so-called nuclear family and the "widow and orphan" for whom our care is not additive but central to our understanding of what the kingdom of God looks like.

3. *We release all things.* Henri Nouwen spoke prophetically when he said the only true prayer is the prayer offered with open hands. Jesus's ministry was one of freedom for hospitality through our availability to others. In this way, the extreme is the normative—we are to sell all, give all, and ultimately receive all as pure gift (Luke 12:33–34 and Mark 10:21, 29–30). To "hold on" and grasp things is harmful—both to relationship with God (consider the "eye of the needle" in Luke 18:18–25) and to one's own identity and relations with others (as we hear in 1 Timothy 6:8–10). It is important to remember that the judgment upon Sodom and Gomorrah was a judgment primarily based upon a lack of hospitality—they had become so consumed with feeding their own lusts and desires that they had no time nor vision to acknowledge the needs of others. In this we as Americans do not stand apart from Sodom, but in its town square.

4. *We are called to desacralize all things.* Jacques Ellul in *The Technological Society* argued that money in and of itself can (often does) hold power over us when we imbue it with idol-like worship.[14] In this way, money *qua* money has quite a bit of power in itself, and we need to act counter to this temptation and set people and relationships in primary consideration as having priority over things. In this way, we need to work toward a redefinition of the good life—not quantity of things but quality of relations. As we are challenged under the divine command ethics of Deuteronomy 5:7, we are not to worship any other God than God . . . period. To hold things and the monetary value we have placed upon those things above drawing people close in relationship with ourselves and their Creator is to choose graven

14. Jacques Ellul, *The Technological Society* (New York: Vintage, 1967).

images. This goes for the notion of usury, or putting interest upon money lent to others. As we hear in 2 Corinthians 8, we are challenged not to coerce more money from people but liberate people from addiction and release people from debts.

5. *As we learn from emancipatory and liberation theologies, God's concern for the poor is central throughout Scripture.* When we become aware of our deep poverty and the poverty of our neighbor, we also discover that our deep poverty is tied to the fate of those who cry from the margins of society. As Ron Sider reminds us:

> Are the people of God truly God's people if they oppress the poor? Is the church really the church if it does not work to free the oppressed? [Regarding Matthew 25:41] The meaning [of Matthew 25] is clear and unambiguous. Jesus intends that disciples imitate his own special concern for the poor and needy. Those who disobey will experience eternal damnation. . . . Regardless of what we do or say on Sunday morning, affluent people who neglect the poor are not the people of God. . . . God is not neutral. His freedom from bias does not mean that he maintains neutrality in the struggle for justice. He is indeed on the side of the poor.[15]

To be on the side of the poor is not to close the door on the middle class or the spiritual poverty of the wealthy. Yet to find the resources to meet the call for God's concern for the materially poor will require centering the priorities and efforts in perhaps new and humble ways that give rise to active love. We are reminded of the Lausanne Covenant Article 9/ 1974: "All of us are shocked by the poverty of millions and disturbed by the injustices which cause it. Those of us who live in affluent circumstances accept our duty to develop a simple lifestyle to contribute more generously to both relief and evangelism."[16] In many

---

15. Ron Sider, *Rich Christians in an Age of Hunger* (London: Hodder and Stoughton, 1990), 70–71.

16. John Stott, The Lausanne Covenant: https://lausanne.org/wp-content/uploads/2021/10/Lausanne-Covenant-%E2%80%93-Pages.pdf, 59–60.

respects, little has changed in the forty years since the Lausanne Covenant was drafted, but the challenge before us as people of integrity, both as Christians in our statements of faith and in our stewardship of resources, is still there. One way we as the church must respond to deep poverty is with the deeper question and response from Micah 6:8: "What does the LORD require of you but to do justice, and to love kindness, and to walk humbly with your God?"

The Challenge of the Church and Academy Is to Develop into a "Community of Loving Defiance"

One of my colleagues in providing feedback for this chapter offered a wonderful "Now what?" question. As he wrote in his comments: "For me, the question is how to translate this message to Millennials so that they can imagine the church addressing their poverty. I don't think they care what Barth, Raschke, Marx, or even Paul thinks. I think they want to *see* a community of people taking care of each other in a deeply troubling world. They aren't looking for answers, but for care. How do we create those communities?"

I honestly couldn't agree more with this insight. When I look to the lives of the young adults I work alongside, I see and feel the weariness in their bodies and souls as they try to navigate the deep poverty that is all around them. More than data sets, their felt need is for mentorship and exemplars in communities. What does it look like to live into a community—and thereby into a life—that is moving away from the deep poverty of our age?

Five Biblical Terms That Call Us out of Deep Poverty and into Active Love

In Hosea 2, we find a deeply passionate call to acknowledge deep poverty and call us to a theological baseline by which to measure what we consider the good life should be. Hosea was written during the eighth century BCE, when Israel was under siege from Assyria and the socioeconomic infrastructure was unravelling. Central to the vision in Hosea is that of a reconciled marriage after infidelity, a call to return to wholeness while acknowledging the excessive brokenness that has befallen the community and social safety nets that have frayed to the point of breaking apart. In chapter 2, God sets yet again the standard of relationship desired and the grounds by which the community can restore itself to wholeness from deep poverty. Using the image of a bride reconciled after infidelity, we hear these words: "And I will take you for my wife forever; I will take you for my wife in righteousness and in justice, in steadfast love, and in mercy. I will take you for my wife in faithfulness; and you shall know the LORD" (Hos. 2:19–20). As Walter Brueggemann makes clear, built within these verses are five terms that are central to addressing the brokenness in Israel's socio-economic and spiritual community and are also applicable to the cries of deep poverty: *Mispat* and *sedeqah*, "justice and righteousness, *hesed*, "steadfast love," *raham*, "mercy," and *amunah*, "faithfulness."[17]

To face the deep poverty in our time and move toward active love, we will need to develop communities of support that help each of us stand firm on the foundation of righteousness, justice, steadfast love, mercy, and faithfulness that God desires. Sider puts it this way: "The church should consist of *communities of loving defiance*. Instead, it consists largely of comfortable clubs of conformity. A far-reaching reformation of the church is a prerequisite if it is to commit itself to Jesus' mission of liberating the oppressed."[18] There is a need for intentionality among the faithful to form a new vision of the church as "communities of loving defiance" since the world is moving with the inertia of consumerism and ego-born appetites that show no natural hope of slowing.[19] The time is now for a spiritual reassess-

17. Walter Brueggemann, *God, Neighbor, Empire: The Excess of Divine Fidelity and the Command of Common Good* (Waco, TX: Baylor University Press, 2016), 12–13.

18. Ron Sider, *Rich Christians in an Age of Hunger*, 200.

19. One way to frame this is to consider the United Nations Sustainable Development Goals (https://undocs.org/E/2019/68) and in particular

ment of economics and the deep poverty where the deficits of the soul are acknowledged on the balance sheet alongside the deficits of the checkbook.

What are some helpful points to actively reflect on as a way forward? Sider uses these criteria for decisions regarding kingdom-centric economics and some helpful points of challenge for young adults today:

- Does this purchase move toward a globally sustainable personal lifestyle?
- How am I distinguishing between necessities and luxuries in my economic priorities?
- Work toward eliminating "status expenditures"—can the jeans I wore last season do the job for this season? Can the iPhone I bought last year do what it needs to do even without more pixels?
- Work toward distinguishing between expenditures for creativity and recreation and excessive self-indulgence.
- Try to encourage expenditures on occasional special celebrations rather than when the whim hits you—i.e., plan ahead for spending.
- Strive toward severing the connection between what you earn and what you consume. This is by far the most difficult task for many. The reality that downsizing is incredibly difficult shouldn't surprise anyone—but the call to do so is certainly central to our faith.

Many of the young adults with whom we worked are already learning to practice some of these out of necessity. They are acutely aware of the deep poverty in our world because, as we have seen, it often affects them the most.

In closing, the challenge before us is to live out an economic program that draws from both a Philippians and Colossians perspective in the face of deep poverty. In the letter to the Philippians, there is

---

goal 12, which is a call to living out a sustainable life with attention to the global responsibility we have to all human flourishing.

that marvelous and breathtaking description of Christ, the son of God, who gave up all aspirations to power in order to be servant of all, emptying (*kenōsis*) himself on the cross. Ministry in the city and the workplace is about being the servant to everyone—the equalizing power of respect. That is the *local* focus of economic responsiveness to deep poverty, where we begin from a kenotic stance by "emptying" ourselves, freeing ourselves from the debt that binds, and walking into the world free to give and free to receive.[20]

The letter to the Colossians speaks of the Christ who is the head of all things and in whom all things hold together. He is the head of the new creation, the church. He is the one who has reconciled all things to himself through the cross. He is the hope of glory within us. Ministry in the city and the workplace is about seeing Jesus as Lord of the city and the systems, as well as the individuals—the empowering vision that means there are no exclusion zones for Christian presence and influence, working to see the "powers that be" honoring the God by whom and for whom they are created. That is the *cosmic* focus.

We acknowledge with confidence the world is God's, as is all that dwells in it—there are no owners, we are all "leasing agents" in creation. As such, we claim the right for marginalized voices in the global market to be not only heard, but listened to, and their words acted upon. Ultimately, we need to have our collective eyes and ears on both the Philippians paradigm and the Colossians mandate. This is living in true stereophonics and responsive economics. It is in the tension of the micro and macro needs of the coming Kingdom of God that we are indeed called and certainly cared for by the gifting hand of God.

Chapter Reflection Questions

1. What is a challenge for you in reforming your approach to more shalom in yourself and in your relationship with the community?

20. Jeffrey F. Keuss, *Freedom of the Self: Kenosis, Cultural Identity and Mission at the Crossroads* (Eugene, OR: Wipf & Stock, 2010).

2. What is something you have discovered from putting the list into practice that may apply to other practices as well?

3. If you no longer consider yourself a young adult, try to access a fear or concern you had as a young adult about your security or safety net. How did that fear or concern shape you for good or for ill? How would you have liked to have made different choices regarding that situation?

4. Of the five terms ("justice," "righteousness," "steadfast love," "mercy," "faithfulness"), which one do you respond to most in this moment or find the most hope in? Why? Which one do you respond to least or makes you most uncomfortable and why?

Appendix

Research Methods

Data for this study was collected through Amazon's Mechanical Turk (MTurk). MTurk is an online marketplace where requesters can post human intelligence tasks (HITs), such as surveys or projects, that individuals can choose to participate in if they meet the qualifications.[1] MTurk was used because we wanted to reach a diverse sample of emerging adults from a broader region of the Pacific Northwest than would be possible by collecting data from local areas. Additionally, we wanted to collect data from emerging adults in the rest of the United States, and MTurk provided access to both samples.

Data collected through MTurk has been compared to using college student or organizational samples.[2] Furthermore, MTurk may provide better data than in-person samples due to its anonymity[3] and

---

1. M. Buhrmeister, T. Kwang, and S. D. Gosling, "Amazon's Mechanical Turk: A New Source of Inexpensive, Yet High-Quality, Data?," *Perspectives on Psychological Science* 6 (2011): 3–5.

2. Sang Eun Woo, Melissa Keith, and Meghan A. Thornton, "Amazon Mechanical Turk for Industrial and Organizational Psychology: Advantages, Challenges, and Practical Recommendations," *Industrial and Organizational Psychology* 8 (2015): 171–79.

3. D. N. Shapiro, J. Chandler, and P. A. Mueller, "Using Mechanical Turk to Study Clinical Populations," *Clinical Psychological Science* 1 (2013): 213–20.

increased diversity.[4] For the purposes of this study, MTurk offered a way to access a more generalizable sample of qualified participants than one collected through a college or religious organization.[5]

For data cleaning, participants were eliminated who failed one or more of the three attention or quality checks, were not in the age range, were not in the specified regions, or did not consent to the use of their data for this research.

4. M. G. Keith and P. D. Harms, "Is Mechanical Turk the Answer to Our Sampling Woes?," *Perspectives on Science and Practice* 9 (2018): 162–67; G. Paolacci and J. Chandler, "Inside the Turk: Understanding Mechanical Turk as a Participant Pool," *Current Directions in Psychological Science* 23 (2014): 184–88.

5. W. R. Shadish, T. D. Cook, and D. T. Campbell, *Experimental and Quasi-experimental Designs for Generalized Causal Inference* (Boston: Houghton Mifflin, 2002).

Contributors

ROBERT DROVDAHL (PhD, Michigan State University) is emeritus professor of educational ministry at Seattle Pacific University. His research interests and publications have focused on human development, educational theory, experiential education, and curriculum design. While completing a forty-four-year career at Seattle Pacific, he also found time to teach intensive courses on ministry leadership in twelve countries in Asia, Africa, South America, and Europe.

MACKENZIE HARRIS (MA, Seattle Pacific University) is completing her PhD in industrial-organizational psychology. She is currently working at a consulting firm in Seattle and plans to use her expertise to coach leaders and make the world of work a better place for employees.

MARTIN JIMÉNEZ (MDiv, Fuller Theological Seminary) is the program director of Pivot NW Research as well as serving as associate pastor of development at Northminster Presbyterian Church (PC[USA]) in North Seattle. When he isn't pushing churches to center young adults in their congregational life, he can be found singing karaoke, playing guitar, or sailing the waterways of the PNW.

JEFFREY F. KEUSS (PhD, University of Glasgow, UK) is professor of Christian ministry, theology, and culture at Seattle Pacific University. He serves as the principal investigator and executive director for Pivot NW Research. An ordained teaching elder in the Presbyterian Church (USA), he is the author of several books and articles looking at the intersection of theology, culture, and the arts as well as young adult innovation in faith communities.

MATHEA KANGAS (MA, Seattle Pacific University) graduated with honors and two bachelor's degrees from the University of Minnesota and was accepted into the PhD program in industrial-organizational psychology at Seattle Pacific. She has since worked with Amazon to develop strategic talent management systems. She divides her free time between writing and exploring the Pacific Northwest.

GABRIELLE METZLER (PhD, Seattle Pacific University) is an industrial-organizational psychologist and learning and excellence manager at Transcarent, a health-care organization focused on developing an ecosystem of high-quality, in-person care and virtual point solutions.

LINDA MONTAÑO (PhD, Seattle Pacific University) is a continuous learner and advocate for individual and community health and well-being. She trains individuals and teams on decent work, financial stewardship, and performance management. She is also the creator of a leading wellness program that fosters belonging, equity, and empowerment throughout the employee life cycle in organizations.

LAUREN ST. MARTIN (MAT, Fuller Theological Seminary) is associate pastor of children, youth, and families at First Covenant Church Seattle. Lauren is also managing editor of *Christ & Cascadia*, an online theology and culture journal housed at the Seattle School of Theology and Psychology. She served on the ethnography team for Pivot NW Research.

Pivot NW Research was founded in 2016 with a generous grant from the Lilly Endowment and is housed in the School of Theology at Seattle Pacific University. The stories, research, and production of this book sprang from the work of the team assembled to discern the specific opportunities and challenges relating to young adults connecting to churches in the Pacific Northwest and the world that God loves.

Works Cited

Adams, Daniel J. "Toward a Theological Understanding of Postmodernism." *Cross Currents* 47, no. 4 (Winter 1997–1998).

Aldefer, Clayton P. *Existence, Relatedness, and Growth: Human Needs in Organizational Settings.* New York: Free Press, 1972.

Anthony, Michael. *Introducing Christian Education: Foundations for the Twenty-First Century.* Grand Rapids: Baker Academic, 2001.

Arnett, Jeffrey J. "College Students as Emerging Adults: The Developmental Implications of the College Context." *Emerging Adulthood* 4, no. 3 (2015).

———. "Emerging Adulthood: A Theory of Development from the Late Teens through the Twenties." *American Psychologist* 55, no. 5 (2000). https://doi.org/10.1037//0003-066x.55.5.469.

———. *Emerging Adulthood: The Winding Road from the Late Teens through the Twenties.* 2nd ed. Oxford: Oxford University Press, 2015.

———. *Emerging Adults in America: Coming of Age in the Twenty-First Century.* Washington, DC: American Psychological Association, 2008.

Augustine, Adam A., and Randy J. Larsen, "Personality, Affect, and Affect Regulation." In *APA Handbook of Personality and Social Psychology.* Vol. 4, *Personality Processes and Individual Differences*, edited by M. Mikulincer, P. R. Shaver, and L. M. Cooper. New York: APA Books, 2015.

Avery, Roger, Frances Goldscheider, and Alden Speare Jr. "Feathered Nest/Gilded Cage: Parental Income and Leaving Home in the Transition to Adulthood." *Demography* 29, no. 3 (1992).

Bandura, Albert. *Social Foundations of Thought and Action: A Social Cognitive Theory.* Englewood Cliffs, NJ: Prentice Hall, 1986.

Barber, Leroy. *Red, Brown, Yellow, Black, White—Who's More Precious in God's Sight? A Call for Diversity in Christian Missions and Ministry.* New York: Jericho Books, 2014.

Bauman, Zygmunt. *Intimations of Postmodernity.* London: Routledge, 1992.

Baumeister, Roy F., and M. R. Leary. "The Need to Belong: Desire for Interpersonal Attachments as a Fundamental Human Motivation." *Psychological Bulletin* 117, no. 3 (1995).

Bee, Helen L., and B. R. Bjorkland. *The Journey of Adulthood.* Hoboken: Prentice Hall, 2000.

Berger, D. O. "On Means, Ends, and Millennials." *Missio Apostolica: Journal of the Lutheran Society for Missiology* 21, no. 41 (2013).

Bishop, Bill. *The Big Sort: Why the Clustering of Like-Minded Americans Is Tearing Us Apart.* Boston: Mariner Books, 2009.

Bonhoeffer, Dietrich. *Letters and Papers from Prison.* London: SCM Press, 2017.

Braun, V., and V. Clarke. "Using Thematic Analysis in Psychology." *Qualitative Research in Psychology* 3 (2006). http://dx.doi.org/10.1191/1478088706qp063oa.

Browne, Ian. "Exploring Reverse Mentoring; 'Win-Win' Relationships in the Multi-generational Workplace." *International Journal of Evidence Based Coaching and Mentoring* 15 (2021).

Brueggemann, Walter. *God, Neighbor, Empire: The Excess of Divine Fidelity and the Command of Common Good.* Waco, TX: Baylor University Press, 2016.

———. *The Prophetic Imagination.* 2nd ed. Minneapolis: Fortress, 2001.

Buber, Martin. "Jewish Religiosity." In *On Judaism: An Introduction to the Essence of Judaism by One of the Most Important Religious Thinkers of the Twentieth Century.* New York: Schocken, 1967.

Buchmann, Marliss. *The Script of Life in Modern Society: Entry into Adulthood in a Changing World.* Chicago: University of Chicago Press, 1989.

Centers for Disease Control and Prevention. "Mental Health Conditions: Anxiety and Depression." CDC website, September 14, 2022. https://www.cdc.gov/tobacco/campaign/tips/diseases/depression-anxiety.html.

Chaudhuri, Sanghamitra, and Rajashi Ghosh. "Reverse Mentoring: A Social Exchange Tool for Keeping the Boomers Engaged and Millennials Committed." *Human Resource Development Review* 11, no. 1 (2012). https://doi.org/10.1177/1534484311417562.

Clydesdale, Tim, and K. Garces-Foley. *The Twentysomething Soul.* Oxford: Oxford University Press, 2019.

Coates, Ta-Nehisi. *Between the World and Me*. New York: Spiegel & Grau, 2015.

Cooper, John W. "Reformed Apologetics and the Challenge of Post-modern Relativism." *Calvin Theological Journal* 28, no. 1 (April 1993).

Cosper, Mike. "Who Killed Mars Hill?" June 21, 2021, in *The Rise and Fall of Mars Hill*, produced by Erik Petrik, podcast. https://www.christianity today.com/ct/podcasts/rise-and-fall-of-mars-hill/who-killed-mars -hill-church-mark-driscoll-rise-fall.html.

De La Torre, Miguel A. *Reading the Bible from the Margins*. Maryknoll, NY: Orbis Books, 2002.

Diener, Ed, R. A. Emmons, R. J. Larsen, and S. Griffin. "The Satisfaction with Life Scale." *Journal of Personality Assessment* 49 (1985).

Dostoevsky, Fyodor. *The Brothers Karamazov*. Translated by Richard Pevear and Larissa Volokhonsky. New York: Farrar, Straus & Giroux, 1990.

Duffy, Ryan D., Bryan J. Dik, Richard P. Douglass, Jessica W. England, and Brandon L. Velez. "Work as a Calling: A Theoretical Model." *Journal of Counseling Psychology* 65, no. 4 (2018).

Eco, Umberto. *Postscript to The Name of the Rose*. Translated by William Weaver. San Diego: Harcourt Brace Jovanovich, 1989.

Ehrhardt, Kyle, and Ellen Ensher. "Perceiving a Calling, Living a Calling, and Calling Outcomes: How Mentoring Matters." *Journal of Counseling Psychology* 68, no. 2 (2021).

Elisabeth Kübler-Ross Foundation. "Kübler-Ross Change Curve." Elisabeth Kübler-Ross Foundation website, 2022. https://www.ekrfoundation .org/5-stages-of-grief/change-curve/.

Ellul, Jacques. *The Technological Society*. New York: Vintage, 1967.

Emerson, Michael O., and Christian Smith. *Divided by Faith: Evangelical Religion and the Problem of Race in America*. Oxford: Oxford University Press, 2001.

Erikson, Erik. *Childhood and Society*. New York: Norton, 1950.

Fiske, S. T. *Social Beings: Core Motives in Social Psychology*. 2nd ed. Hoboken, NJ: John Wiley & Sons, 2010.

Fosner, Verlon. *Dinner Church: Building Bridges by Breaking Bread*. Franklin, TN: Seedbed Publishing, 2017.

Fowler, James W. *Stages of Faith: The Psychology of Human Development and the Quest for Meaning*. New York: HarperOne, 1995.

Frankl, Viktor E. *Man's Search for Meaning*. New York: Simon and Schuster, 1985.

Frey, William H. "The Millennial Generation: A Demographic Bridge to

America's Diverse Future." The Brookings Institution website, January 2018. http://www.brookings.edu/research/millennials.

Fry, Richard. "Five Facts about Millennial Households." Pew Research Center website, September 6, 2017. https://www.pewresearch.org/fact-tank/2017/09/06/5-facts-about-millennial-households/.

Gallup Inc. "How Millennials Want to Work and Live." Report, 2016. https://www.gallup.com/workplace/238073/millennials-work-live.aspx.

George, L. K., D. B. Larson, H. G. Koenig, and M. E. McCullough. "Spirituality and Health: What We Know, What We Need to Know." *Journal of Social and Clinical Psychology* 19 (2000).

Goldman, Ronald. *Religious Thinking from Childhood to Adolescence*. New York: Seabury Press, 1968.

Goodman, Fallon R., David J. Disabato, Todd B. Kashdan, Scott B. Kauffman. "Measuring Well-Being: A Comparison of Subjective Well-Being and PERMA." *The Journal of Positive Psychology* 13, no. 4 (2018). https://doi.org/10.1080/17439760.2017.1388434.

Grant, Adam M., and Sabine Sonnentag. "Doing Good Buffers against Feeling Bad: Prosocial Impact Compensates for Negative Task and Self-Evaluations." *Organizational Behavior and Human Decision Processes* 111, no. 1 (2010).

Hall, G. Stanley. *Adolescence: Its Psychology and Its Relations to Physiology, Anthropology, Sociology, Sex, Crime, Religion and Education*. New York: Appleton, 1904.

Hardie, Jessica, Lisa Pearce, and Melinda Denton. "The Dynamics and Correlates of Religious Service Attendance in Adolescence." *Youth & Society* 48, no. 2 (2013). https://doi.org/10.1177/0044118X13483777.

Heschel, Abraham J. *The Sabbath*. New York: Farrar, Straus & Giroux, 1951.

Ilgen, Daniel R., Cynthia D. Fisher, and Susan M. Taylor. "Consequences of Individual Feedback on Behavior in Organizations." *Journal of Applied Psychology* 64, no. 4 (1979). https://doi-org/10.1037/0021-9010.64.4.349.

Inbody, Tyron. "Postmodernism: Intellectual Velcro Dragged across Culture." *Theology Today* 57, no. 4 (January 1995).

James, Chris. *Church Planting in Post-Christian Soil*. Oxford: Oxford University Press, 2018.

Jay, Meg. *The Defining Decade: Why Your Twenties Matter and How to Make the Most of Them Now*. New York: Twelve, 2012.

Jensen, Lene A., and Jeffrey J. Arnett. "Going Global: New Pathways for

Adolescents and Emerging Adults in a Changing World." *Journal of Social Issues* 68, no. 3 (2012).

Kaemingk, Matthew. "Pacific Northwest Religion: Doing It Different, Doing It Alone, Part 1." Christ & Cascadia website. October 25, 2013. https://christandcascadia.com/2013/10/25/religion-in-the-pacific-northwest-doing-it-different/.

Keuss, Jeffrey F. *Freedom of the Self: Kenosis, Cultural Identity and Mission at the Crossroads.* Eugene, OR: Wipf & Stock, 2010.

Killen, Patricia O'Connell, and Mark Silk. *Religion and Public Life in the Pacific Northwest: The None Zone.* Lanham, MD: AltaMira Press, 2004.

Kohlberg, Lawrence. "Stages of Moral Development as a Basis for Moral Education." *Harvard Educational Review* 34, no. 1 (1964).

Kotter, John P. "Leading Change: Why Transformation Efforts Fail." *Harvard Business Review* 73, no. 2 (1995).

Krogstad, Mathea., G. Metzler, P. Yost, J. Keuss, and M. Allison. "Beyond the Pews: A Multidimensional Approach to Young Adults' Faith Development." Unpublished manuscript, 2022.

Kuk-Won, Shin. "Postmodernism and a Christian Response." *Pro Rege* 22, no. 4 (June 1994). http://www.dordt.edu/publications/pro_rege/crcpi/95097.pdf.

Leong, David. *Race and Place: How Urban Geography Shapes the Journey to Reconciliation.* Downers Grove, IL: IVP Books, 2017.

Levinson, Daniel J. *The Seasons of Man's Life.* New York: Knopf, 1978.

Lloyd, Sarah Anne. "New Seattle Apartments Have Shrunk Almost 30% in 15 Years." *Curbed Seattle.* November 2, 2017. https://seattle.curbed.com/2017/11/2/16599858/seattle-apartment-size-shrinking-data.

Luedke, Courtney L., D. L. McCoy, R. Winkle-Wagner, and J. Lee-Johnson. "Students Perspectives on Holistic Mentoring Practices in STEM Fields." *JCSCORE* 5, no. 1 (2019).

Lugo, Luis. "Religion among the Millennials: Less Religiously Active than Older Americans, but Fairly Traditional in Other Ways." A Pew Forum on Religion & Public Life Report. 2010. http://assets.pewresearch.org/wp-content/uploads/sites/11/2010/02/millennials-report.pdf.

Manglos-Weber, Nicolette. "Relationships with God among Young Adults: Validating a Measurement Model with Four Dimensions." *Sociology of Religion* 77, no. 2 (2016).

Mary, Aurélie A. "Re-evaluating the Concept of Adulthood and the Framework of Transition." *Journal of Youth Studies* 17 (2014).

Maslow, Abraham H. *Motivation and Personality*. New York: Harper & Row, 1954.

Maton, Kenneth I. "The Stress-Buffering Role of Spiritual Support: Cross-Sectional and Prospective Investigations." *Journal for the Scientific Study of Religion* 28 (1989).

McClelland, David C. *The Achieving Society*. New York: Van Nostrand, 1961.

Mercadante, Linda. A. *Belief without Borders: Inside the Minds of the Spiritual but Not Religious*. New York: Oxford University Press, 2014.

Merritt, Carol H. *The Tribal Church: Ministering to the Missing Generation*. Herndon, VA: The Alban Institute, 2007.

Merton, Thomas. *Conjectures of a Guilty Bystander*. Garden City, NY: Image Books, 1966.

———. "Contemplation in a World of Action." In *Thomas Merton: Spiritual Master*. New York: Paulist Press, 1992.

———. *Life and Holiness*. New York: Herder & Herder, 1963.

———. *Seeds of Destruction*. New York: Farrar, Straus & Giroux, 1964.

———. *The Silent Life*. New York: Farrar, Straus & Giroux, 1999.

———. *Wisdom of the Desert*. New York: New Directions, 1960.

Metzler, Gabrielle, M. Krogstad, P. Yost, J. Keuss, M. Allison, and K. Hemphill. "Faith Community Differentiators: The Unique Role of Faith Communities for Young Adults." Unpublished manuscript, 2022.

Morgan, Teresa. *Roman Faith and Christian Faith: Pistis and Fides in the Early Roman Empire and Early Churches*. Oxford: Oxford University Press, 2017.

Murray, Charles. *Coming Apart: The State of White America, 1960–2010*. New York: Crown Forum, 2012.

———. *The Bell Curve: Intelligence and Class Structure in American Life*. New York: Free Press, 1994.

Pargament, Kenneth I. "The Bitter and the Sweet: An Evaluation of the Costs and Benefits of Religiousness." *Psychological Inquiry* 13 (2002).

Pazmiño, Robert W. *Foundational Issues in Christian Education: An Introduction in Evangelical Perspective*. Grand Rapids: Baker, 1988.

Pearce, Lisa, and Melinda Denton. "A Faith of Their Own: Stability and Change in the Religiosity of America's Adolescents." *Contemporary Sociology* 31, no. 3 (2012).

———. *A Faith of Their Own: Stability and Change in the Religiosity of America's Adolescents*. New York: Oxford University Press, 2011.

Pelikan, Jaroslav. *The Vindication of Tradition: The 1983 Jefferson Lectures on the Humanities*. New Haven, CT: Yale University Press, 1986.

Pew Research Center, "America's Changing Religious Landscape." Pew Research Center website, May 12, 2015. https://www.pewresearch.org/religion/2015/05/12/americas-changing-religious-landscape/.

Pivot NW Research. "Young Adults and the Church in the Pacific Northwest and U.S.: 2017–2018 Study." Pivot NW Research website, retrieved November 23, 2019. https://pivotnw.org/research.

Prilleltensky, Isaac. "Mattering at the Intersection of Psychology, Philosophy, and Politics." *American Journal of Community Psychology* 65 (2020). https://doi.org/10.1002/ajcp.12368.

Pustulka, Paula, J. Sarnowska, and M. Buler. "Resources and Pace of Leaving Home among Young Adults in Poland." *Journal of Youth Studies* (2021). https://doi.org/10.1080/13676261.2021.1925638.

Putnam, Robert D. *Our Kids: The American Dream in Crisis*. New York: Simon & Schuster, 2015.

Raschke, Carl. *The Next Reformation: Why Evangelicals Must Embrace Postmodernity*. Grand Rapids: Baker Academic, 2004.

Ryff, C. D. "Happiness Is Everything, or Is It? Explorations on the Meaning of Psychological Well-Being." *Journal of Personality and Social Psychology* 57 (1989).

———. "Psychological Well-Being in Adult Life." *Current Directions in Psychological Science* 4 (1995).

Sage Data. "Average Age of Mother from the Births Data Summary Database." Sage Data website. https://doi.org/10.6068/DP17B1319A2F08.

Seattle Department of Neighborhoods. "Rainier Beach Neighborhood Snapshot." City of Seattle website, August 2019. http://www.seattle.gov/Documents/Departments/Neighborhoods/Districts/Neighborhood%20Snapshots/Rainier-Beach-Snapshot.pdf.

Setran, David P. *Spiritual Formation in Emerging Adulthood: A Practical Theology for College and Young Adult Ministry*. Grand Rapids: Baker Academic, 2013.

Settersten, Richard A., et al. "Understanding the Effects of COVID-19 Through a Life Course Lens." *Advances in Life-Course Research* (2020). https://doi.org/10.1016/j.alcr.2020.100360.

Shelton, Delia S., M. M. Delgado, E. V. G. Greenway, E. A. Hobson, A. C. R. Lackey, A. Medina-García, B. A. Reinke, P. A. Trillo, C. P. Wells, and M. C. Horner-Devine. "Expanding the Landscape of Opportunity: Professional Societies Support Early-Career Researchers through Community Programming and Peer Coaching." *Journal of*

Comparative Psychology 135, no. 4 (2021). https://doi.org/10.1037/com0000300.

Shoda, Yuichi, Nicole L. Wilson, Donna D. Whitsett, Jenna Lee-Dussud, and Vivian Zayas. "The Person as a Cognitive-Affective Processing System: Quantitative Ideography as an Integral Component of Cumulative Science." In *APA Handbook of Personality and Social Psychology*. Vol. 4, *Personality Processes and Individual Differences*, edited by M. Mikulincer, P. R. Shaver, and L. M. Cooper. New York: APA Books, 2015.

Sider, Ron. *Rich Christians in an Age of Hunger*. London: Hodder and Stoughton, 1990.

Simmons, Brian. *Wandering in the Wilderness: Changes and Challenges to Emerging Adults' Christian Faith*. Abilene, TX: Abilene Christian University Press, 2011.

Smith, Christian, K. M. Hojara, H. A. Davidson, and P. S. Herzog. *Lost in Transition: The Dark Side of Emerging Adulthood*. New York: Oxford University Press, 2011.

Soerens, Tim. *Everywhere You Look: Discovering the Church Right Where You Are*. Downers Grove, IL: InterVarsity Press, 2020.

Steele, Les L. *On the Way: A Practical Theology of Christian Formation*. Grand Rapids: Baker, 1990.

Steger, M. F., and B. J. Dik. "Work as Meaning: Individual and Organizational Benefits of Engaging in Meaningful Work." In *Oxford Handbook of Positive Psychology and Work*, edited by P. A. Linley, S. Harrington, and N. Page. Oxford: Oxford University Press, 2010.

Steger, M. F., P. Frazier, S. Oishi, and M. Kaler. "The Meaning in Life Questionnaire: Assessing the Presence of and Search for Meaning in Life." *Journal of Counseling Psychology* 53 (2006).

Steiner, George. *Nostalgia for the Absolute*. Toronto: House of Anansi Press, 1974.

Stott, John. The Lausanne Covenant: Complete Text and Study Guide. https://lausanne.org/wp-content/uploads/2021/10/Lausanne-Covenant-%E2%80%93-Pages.pdf.

Tanyi, R. A. "Towards Clarification of the Meaning of Spirituality." *Journal of Advanced Nursing* 39 (2002).

Taylor, John Vernon. *Enough Is Enough*. London: SCM, 1975.

Thurston, Angie, and Casper ter Kuile. "How We Gather: The Rise of Unaffiliated Millennials." Harvard Divinity School and Crestwood Foundation Report, 2015. https://caspertk.files.wordpress.com/2015/04/how-we-gather1.pdf.

Tillich, Paul. "On the Idea of a Theology of Culture." In *What Is Religion?* Translated by James L. Adams. New York: Harper & Row, 1969.

Twenge, J. M, A. B. Cooper, T. E. Joiner, M. E. Duffy, and S. G. Binau. "Age, Period, and Cohort Trends in Mood Disorder Indicators and Suicide-Related Outcomes in a Nationally Representative Dataset, 2005–2017." *Journal of Abnormal Psychology* 128, no. 3 (2019). https://doi.org/10.1037/abn0000410.

Twenge, Jean M., and Stacy M. Campbell. "Generational Differences in Psychological Traits and Their Impact on the Workplace." *Journal of Managerial Psychology* 23 (2008).

United Nations Economic & Social Counsel. "Progress towards the Sustainable Development Goals." UN Digital Library, May 8, 2019. https://digitallibrary.un.org/record/3810131?ln=en.

US Census Bureau. "Figure MS-2 Median Age at First Marriage: 1890 to Present." 2022. https://www.census.gov/content/dam/Census/library/visualizations/time-series/demo/families-and-households/ms-2.pdf.

———. "Highest Educational Attainment Levels since 1940." https://www.census.gov/library/visualizations/2017/comm/cb17-51_educational_attainment.html.

———. "Statistical Abstract of the United States: 2021." https://www.census.gov/library/publications/2011/compendia/statab/131ed.html.

Volf, Miroslav. *Exclusion and Embrace: A Theological Exploration of Identity, Otherness, and Reconciliation.* Nashville: Abingdon, 1996.

Waters, Richard D., and Denise Sevick Bortree. "Can We Talk about the Direction of This Church? The Impact of Responsiveness and Conflict on Millennials' Relationship with Religious Institutions." *Journal of Media and Religion* 11, no. 4 (2012).

Wilson, Ceri, and Jennifer Stock. "The Impact of Living with Long-Term Conditions in Young Adulthood on Mental Health and Identity: What Can Help?" *Health Expect* 22 (2019). https://doi.org/10.1111/hex.12945.

Winogrodzka, Dominika, and Izabela Grabowska. "(Dis)ordered Social Sequences of Mobile Young Adults: Spatial, Social and Return Mobilities." *Journal of Youth Studies* (2021). https://doi.org/10.1080/1367 6261.2020.1865526.

Zuckerman, Phil, Luke W. Galen, and Frank L. Pasquale. *The Nonreligious: Understanding Secular People and Societies.* New York: Oxford University Press, 2016.

Index